streams run
UPHILL

CONVERSATIONS with young
clergywomen of color

MIHEE KIM-KORT, EDITOR

Foreword by Marvin A. McMickle
Afterword by Rhashell Hunter

JUDSON PRESS
PUBLISHERS SINCE 1824
VALLEY FORGE, PA

Interior design by Crystal Devine, Devine Design.
Cover design by Wendy Ronga, Hampton Design Group.

Library of Congress Cataloging-in-Publication data
Cataloging-in-Publication Data available upon request.
Contact cip@judsonpress.com.

Printed in the U.S.A.

First Edition, 2014.

To all those women,
the mothers, the writers, the artists, and the prophets,
who are an oasis
and who stir up a fresh vision of God's kingdom with
    their work and lives
so that we might continue faithfully in this journey.

5/23/14

Keila,

Many Congratulations! So,
proud of you persevering!
may the Lord bless you and
keep you especially now as
you discover next steps. I
trust and know God has
great plans for you and
your family! ¡adelante!
Yana

contents

foreword

The words of Ephesians 4:11 seem to flow so easily, so effortlessly, so expectantly: "God called some to be apostles, some prophets, some evangelists, and some pastors and teachers...." If there were to be any restrictions or limitations placed upon who was qualified to be called into any of these offices, this would have been a good place to state them. God called some—except women. God called some—except certain ethnic or language groups. God called some—except those deemed by someone to be too young or too old. God called some—except LGBTQ persons. God called some—except unmarried persons. God called some—except single women with children. All that the writer of Ephesians did was establish the offices and positions that God needed to have filled if the church is to accomplish its ministries in the world. It is people in the church, more informed by cultural norms and personal prejudices than by solid exegesis or sound theology that have tried to set limits on who is qualified for a leadership position in their church.

The truth and power of *Streams Run Uphill* is that it is not an argument with any verse(s) of Scripture. It is not another effort to read and interpret 1 Corinthians 14:34-35 or 1 Timothy 2:11-12 in a twenty-first century, postmodern context. Rather, this book is a collection of reflections from young clergywomen of color, whose resistance to their call to ministry comes not from the Bible but from their own churches, not from God but from persons within their own communities. They are, all of them, convinced that God has called them into some form of Christian ministry. The uphill struggle is not the result of their swimming against the will of the Holy Spirit. Rather, they swim uphill as they struggle to overcome the sexism, racism, and ageism that are thrown before them as obstacles to God's calling.

I wonder if people in the church have any idea how much pain we inflict upon people who are guilty of nothing more than answering God's call to ministry? The cries of anguish and the stories of exclusion or limitation are not uniform by any means. The voices in this book are Asian, Latina, African, and African American. Within each of those groups, there are still more layers of diversity; Presbyterian, American Baptist, and Pan African Orthodox Church. Despite these differences in denomination and self-description, one thing remains the same: someone has tried to prevent these women from pursuing the call that God has laid upon them. More precisely, that attempt at exclusion is not based upon preparation or competence. Rather, it is based upon gender, ethnicity, language group, or age.

It has become painfully obvious that women in ministry are faced with limitations and assumptions altogether unknown to most of their male colleagues. I announced my call to ministry at the age of 16, and no one in my church told me I was too young to speak of such things. I was ordained at age 25 and installed in my first pastoral assignment of 600 members when 28 years old. My career took the trajectory that every member of the clergy might desire: the call to a larger, metropolitan, more prestigious pulpit. I was given every opportunity to exercise my gifts in denominational, ecumenical, and theological gatherings. No one ever told me no when I sought to make full proof of my ministry.

I was not assigned to a rural congregation or to a small church with a handful of aging members where none of my male colleagues was willing or even required to go. I was not locked into a role as assistant to the pastor, or locked out of a senior pastorate, based solely upon my gender or my ethnicity or my age. I was not confronted with some convoluted exegesis by clergy colleagues who were absolutely convinced that, while other aspects of first century AD life in Palestine and Asia Minor were no longer binding on a twenty-first century North American church, the prohibition against women in ministry was meant to stand forever.

Reading this book, *Streams Run Uphill*, just reminds me of the difference between how I was treated when I began in ministry and how my sisters in ministry have been and continue to be treated in the church. Reading this book made me angry over those differences in treatment. Reading this book made me weep as I listened to and grieved with those whom God has called but whom the church has too often obstructed or altogether rejected. Reading this book made me determined to use every avenue, every outlet, and every opportunity available to me to push back against the sexism, racism, and ageism that lie at the heart of these stories of courage and perseverance.

I must offer a disclosure at this point: my first pastor as a child while growing up in Chicago, Illinois, was a woman. She was the Reverend Dr. Mary G. Evans, pastor of the Cosmopolitan Community Church. She is one of the women featured in *Daughters of Thunder* by Betty Collier-Thomas. Trained at Payne Theological Seminary where she graduated in 1911, Pastor Evans also studied at Union Theological Seminary and Columbia University in New York City. She was awarded an honorary Doctor of Divinity by Wilberforce University. She served as pastor of our church for thirty-five years. When she died in 1966, the church had 600 members. From my birth in 1948 until we moved far away from the neighborhood in which the church was located in 1957, hers was the only preaching voice I knew. You can imagine what a shock it was for me when I was later informed by male clergy of much less training, talent, or accomplishment than Pastor Evans that God did not call women to be preachers.

I commend this book to several groups of readers. First, to all young clergywomen of color, so that you will know that you are not alone in your struggles to overcome sexism, racism, and ageism in the church. Next, to male clergy of all ages, denominations, ethnicities, and languages, so that you will hear the heart and the hopes of your sisters in the service of the Lord. Female clergy should not and must not be the only persons advocating for their full inclusion in the ministry of the church. There is an urgent need for male advocates as well; more specifically there is a need for male clergy who understand how wrong it is to deny women the very rights and privileges that male clergy have always taken for granted for themselves.

Finally, I hope many lay women will read this book and come to embrace more fully the aspirations of other women for careers in ministry. It is not lost on any of the writers in this book that it is not just male members of the clergy and the laity who have tried to block and obstruct women in their pursuit of the ministries to which God has called them. For whatever reasons (and those reasons vary from biblical interpretation to cultural norms), a great many women in churches all across the country and all around the world have been slow to embrace the idea of women in ministry. How odd that women can celebrate every time another woman breaks through a glass ceiling in politics, athletics, business, education, or the arts. However, when it comes to the church, a strange resistance takes over in the minds of too many women and they begin to trumpet the notion that women have no place in the pulpit.

The title of this book echoes the struggles that are recorded inside: gifted and committed young women of color struggling to answer their call to ministry in the name of the One of whom it was said: "Can any good thing come out of Nazareth?" Something good did come out of Nazareth, to the dismay and shock of many. Similarly, there are many good things that await those that take the time to read this book. Because this isn't only a collection of stories about struggle; it is also a groundswell of stories about resilient faith, of enduring hope, of unflinching love, and of abiding joy. These women find encouragement in sharing their stories, and we can celebrate their strength of purpose and the divine authority that bolsters their call. Hopefully the time will soon come when women in ministry will no longer be such an uphill struggle. As a son of Mary G. Evans, that is my fervent hope and prayer!

Marvin A. McMickle, PhD
President
Professor of Church Leadership
Colgate Rochester Crozer Divinity School

prologue

Where streams run uphill, there a woman rules. —ETHIOPIAN
PROVERB

I cannot recall where I first saw these words. But I knew it was
more than just a pithy statement or a perplexing but lovely image,
so I wrote it down immediately into a journal. I wanted to let the
words roll over me again and again and give myself time and space
to soak up the gorgeous tension of these words. The contradictions
and clash of realities compelled me to soak myself in this image.
I felt a power and truth here not only for my identity as a human
being, and specifically as a woman, but also for what it could mean
for me as a clergywoman, and a clergywoman of color. Something
from deep within this proverb filled and nourished what had been
empty and dry for much too long.

So, I drank from its well in huge draughts. I washed myself in
it. I swam in it. Memories and stories emerged as the image of water drew me into its soothing whirlpools and eddies. I remembered
fishing trips with my father, and the first time I caught a fish how it
was my mother who enthusiastically helped me reel it in. I imagined
the Israelites stumbling along on that muddy path through the Red
Sea, mesmerized by the rush of waterfalls on either side of such a
precarious but strange and wonderful journey. I saw the creeks I
hiked along in Colorado that were nestled among cliffs and peaks,
terrifying and beautiful, but despite the majesty of those mountains
how my eyes always turned down and stayed on the quiet, moving water. I heard God's voice calling out to Jesus as he stood up,

vulnerable and drenched in the waters of John's baptism, calling out those words of love, and I felt those divine words in my bones, too. I felt the undercurrent of the first ocean where I dove and turned like a fish, and it made me think of all those oceans—the Pacific, the Atlantic, and the Caribbean—that baptized me, too.

But it is the dynamic but unexpected harmony of streams that "run uphill" that compels me the most. There is struggle in an uphill endeavor, but miracle in its very existence. There is an irrationality about it, as well as a subversive, kingdom-shaking quality. There is something off-putting and hard to swallow but undeniably compelling about it. So, too, it is with the "other" clergywomen and our work and ministry, their calling and community relationships, their voices and their perspectives. There is a necessity for their ministries and their stories, a need more pressing now than ever.

I had the opportunity to tell my own story and my theology, but I found myself desperate to uncover the meaningful and therefore pertinent experiences of the rare but growing number of other clergywomen. They are the other in that they are non-Anglo. They are seen as exotic, foreign, and mysterious. Some have accents. Some look and sound "American." Some look incredibly young. Some are bilingual. Some are quiet. Some are vociferous. Some are incredible preachers. Some have a healing pastoral presence. Some are mothers. Some are single. Some are gay. Some are recent immigrants. Some are second or third generation. They serve in Asian American, African American, and Spanish-speaking congregations, or, like me, they serve congregations that look nothing like them. I hunger for the life-giving words that came from our unique calling and the acknowledgment of the distinct challenges we faced from the moment we decided to say, "Lord, here I am. Send me."

And so, we have this gathering, each clergywoman making not only waves and ripples but also currents, and moving not only mountains but also whole oceans with their voices, lives, and ministries, their own theologies, some in rhythm with each other like waves lapping the shore, and some in honest but equally meaningful collisions, crashing against the rocks of varying obstacles and challenges. There are narratives and lessons about confronting the distracting length of our hair, the surprising youthfulness in our faces, the softness of our accented voices, the family and children always clinging to our robes, the uncertainty about our voices, authority, and calling. There are stories about the heavy burden we carry because of the color of our skin and what it means to confront our identity with congregations that both contrast with us and mirror us. There are words about what we have gleaned from our own lives—hard lessons, and ones that continue to surprise us season after season.

I remember from a seminary class the words of our *mujerista* sister theologians: *La vida es la lucha*. Life is a struggle. Despite the distinctive quality of these stories, what ties us together, and with all our sisters around the world, is the struggle. We claw. We scuffle. We rise, tooth and nail, tear-soaked and blood-spilled in it all. But it is not only the hardships, the obstacles, and conflicts; it is also the miracles. It is the miracle and wonder, the undeniable beauty of grace we encounter in ourselves and in our callings. We overcome much. We surmount even more. We triumph over the impossible. Yet, even more importantly, while much of the journey is uphill, the promise of God in community is that we never journey alone. We share each other's burdens. We carry each other on our shoulders. We hold each other's tears. And so, I hope it is with these words: that they would remind us of our shared baptism, the promise and proclamation of God's claiming us, and how that is the most important voice in our lives, and one that comes to us and we hear in this community.

And in that sharing, we hear and know God's unquenchable love for us and press on all the more.

Women have no
beginning
only continual
flows.

Though rivers flow
women are not
rivers.

Women are not
roses
they are not oceans
or stars.

I would like to tell
her this but
I think she
already knows.

—Ana Castillo, "Women Are Not Roses"

introduction

BRIDGETT A. GREEN

We are each gifted in a unique and important way. It is our privilege and our adventure to discover our own special light.

—MARY DUNBAR

Streams Run Uphill: Conversations with Young Clergywomen of Color is a resource for young women of color who are discerning ministry as their vocation. This collection of essays describes experiences, struggles, and triumphs of young clergywomen of color serving churches and communities in different denominations across the United States. While celebrating the call into ministry, it offers deep and critical reflections of the struggles that come when streams run uphill.

The aim of this project is to encourage, support, and advocate. It encourages young women of color in their call to ministry by sharing stories from women who may look and talk like them. It supports young clergywomen of color in their current calls with insights and reflections that affirm that they are not alone. And it advocates for support of young clergywomen of color as they grow in ministry. In addition to reassuring readers that such young clergywomen exist, this book offers stories of struggles and triumphs that testify to the gift of ministry and their gifts for ministry.

When the fingertip of God grazes the soul with a call for ordained Christian ministry, a divine spark ignites our sense of purpose and exhilaration courses through our veins. We begin to understand God's desire for us to serve, encourage, edify, comfort, and convict our communities and ourselves to be the hands and feet of Christ. But as young women of color, we see that hardly anyone called to ordained ministry looks like us, talks like us, and has had experiences similar to ours. And then we are stuck. We are stuck with social and ecclesial scripts that ministry is for men, that ministry is best done by white clergy, or that ministry is for older people who have more life experiences.

THE UPHILL CLIMB:
social realities of clergywomen of color

Ministering as a young woman of color is no crystal stair. Unlike most men, women do not receive unanimous support from their communities and their churches. For many, models of female ministers, particularly those who serve as pastors or heads of staff in congregations, are uncommon in most Protestant congregations, especially because many of them do not ordain women as clergy. As of 2000, the Southern Baptist Convention stopped ordaining women as clergy. As of 2009, only 10 percent of senior pastors of Protestant congregations across the denominational spectrum are women.[1]

In denominations where women's ordination is constitutional, women still experience various forms of discrimination. Many Protestant denominations, including the PC(USA), the United Methodist Church (UMC), the Evangelical Lutheran Church of America (ELCA), the United Church of Christ (UCC), the Episcopal Church, and various Baptist conventions, do have female clergy. In general, these clergywomen struggle against inequalities based on gender. The *New York Times* reported that many people in the pew have difficulty in seeing women as religious authority figures.[2] Clergywomen confront challenges in ministry placement, with being treated as inferior to men, with inequity in pay, and with limited opportunities for promotion and growth in ministry.[3]

In addition to sexism in ministry, racism undermines experience of greater richness in doing ministry for clergywomen of color. To be a woman of color is not simply a descriptor of women who are African American, Asian American, Latina, Middle Eastern American, or Native American. The term "of color" also expresses the racialization[4] of those in the United States who are not privileged by the social construct of whiteness. For example, in the PC(USA), many women of color profess a deep love for Jesus and for the denomination while confessing their struggles with the church's treatment of them as outsiders.[5] An example of racism in ecclesial structures includes the limited participation of racialized people in general, and racialized women in particular, in national conventions and regional meetings where denominational polity, policy, and theological doctrines are developed.[6] Clergywomen of color experience racism differently from men and sexism differently from white clergywomen.

Because young adults (ages 35 and younger, or even age 40 and younger) naturally have less life experience than their older colleagues, young clergywomen of color also are confronted by ageism. Veteran clergy often equate youthful years with deficiency in leadership and inexperience in vocation. (Conversely, second- or third-career clergy, who are new to ordained ministry but seasoned in years, are also dismissed or devalued based on their elder status.) Although it is likely that young clergy have less professional and possibly ministerial experience than do older clergy, young clergy still have many gifts and skills that are valuable to the life of the church. Their perspectives can help to shape a vision for future ministries that they will continue to lead. Underestimation of young adults' experience, body of knowledge, and different modes of operating contribute to the hemorrhaging of young adults from congregations and undermines young clergywomen's ability to live fully into their calls.[7]

FORMING NEW GROUND

Sexism, racism, and ageism are a few of the elements that make young women's leadership challenging. However, even as the stream runs uphill, the stream is flowing with God's help, nurturing the lands, animals, and people along the way. This project testifies to the various experiences of young clergywomen who cherish the gifts without denying the struggle of being called.

In chapters 1–3, the writers offer perspective on sexism, racism, and ageism. In many cultures, the struggle with oppression based on gender roles is still prevalent. In Christian communities, whether

Anglo or not, it seems that this is perpetuated by attitudes toward women's roles in the church. For those who are visibly non-Anglo, negotiating this issue is often unsettling and even frustrating. It is difficult to navigate the issues of racial difference, especially in churches where a clergywoman of color serves an Anglo congregation. Even in the wider community, where the pastor plays a public role, this can pose a barrier. Rather than rejecting womanhood, one way to confront this issue is through the embrace of one's femininity and allowing it to be an expression of the Divine, both within and without the church walls. This approach can also make way for positive dialogue about reconciliation.

Ageism is difficult to pin down in terms of description and perhaps is one of the most difficult matters to overcome because of the generally dismissive attitude toward both younger and older women. "You look just like one of the kids!" is a sentiment expressed often to ministers to youth. "How does she have the energy to do ministry?" is asked of those who are second-career clergywomen. These kinds of comments are condescending toward clergywomen of any age.

Chapters 4–6 incorporate engagement of all the aforementioned factors. For instance, chapter 4 describes ways in which community might be embodied and lived out. Often, in a community where the clergywoman is a minority, she may struggle to find ways to connect with that community. People naturally bond over shared lifestyles and interests, and especially cultural traditions. For a young clergywoman of color, this can feel isolating, so it becomes necessary to find ways to intersect with the community by sharing in local traditions, as well as freely sharing one's own passions and cultural heritage. In chapter 5, tokenism, which is often a backlash of cultural diversity, is examined. Sometimes it is presumed that the clergywoman of color needs to assimilate into the local culture in order to be heard or understood by congregation members. In chapter 6, the author reflects on ways of navigating the expectations of family and the difficulty of balancing all these roles. One's ethnic or cultural background also plays a role in shaping the identity of parent and pastor.

Chapters 7–9 engage the tangibles of ministry and calling. In chapter 7, we read about how being the other pastor is difficult whether one is an associate, assistant, or parish associate. Here are honest stories about the difficulties, and the authors address the ways one can deal with being the other—not only the other pastor—through honest communication, staff support, and persistent establishing of oneself. Chapter 8 includes stories about how clergywomen often find themselves in generalist positions where there are many duties ranging from youth and children's ministry to pastoral care. These are opportunities to discover one's passions, whether for evangelism and mission or for hospital visitations. But how does one negotiate all the expectations and duties while still making time to explore interests? For clergywomen of color this may include incorporating their experiences of racism and sexism in their ministry pursuits. Chapter 9 addresses the ways one can live into one's voice and use one's voice courageously to express authority.

The last chapter offers testimonies of those who have gone through the calling process and includes stories of obstacles, victories, rejections, and conclusions about calling and the way it is experienced uniquely but powerfully for women of color.

For the most part, each chapter is written by one author, but interwoven throughout each section are stories of other clergywomen and their engagement of the issues. Because it is impossible to offer only one piece of wisdom or advice, it makes sense to present the multifaceted and multidimensional ways in which clergywomen of color—each of whom is rooted in her unique ethnic heritage—provide perspective. There is some overlap. There is some contradiction. But there is always a word of encouragement and edification. That ties all of it together—every woman of color is a woman and a human being, and that in itself is a universally reliable ground from which to work for the church.

Each chapter provides a wider framework in which the clergywoman shares her story, experiences, and epiphanies while leaving space for stories to come out of other contexts. These essays are an invitation to ponder, reflect, and supplement the larger story of grace and calling with our own stories.

Notes

1. Barna Group, "Number of Female Senior Pastors in Protestant Churches Doubles in Past Decade," 2009.

2. Neela Banerjee, "Clergywomen Find Hard Path to Bigger Pulpit," *New York Times* online, 2006.

3. In the UMC, for example, most clergywomen of color serve in congregations. Yet, in a survey, these clergywomen shared concerns regarding sufficient salary support and lack of support for promotion within their ecclesial system. Jung Ha Kim and Rosetta Ross, "The Status of Racial and Ethnic Minority Clergywomen in the United Methodist Church," The General Board of Higher Education and Ministry, 2004.

4. Racialization is a process in which groups of people are deemed to be inferior based on biological phenotypes and presumed culture by a ruling group that uses social, political, and legal structures to legitimate and maintain discrimination, inequality, and limited access to material goods, political influence, and social well-being.

5. Presbyterian Church (USA), *Hearing and Singing New Songs to God: Shunning Old Discords and Sharing New Harmonies*, Report of the Women of Color Consultation Task Force to the 218th General Assembly, 2008. Women of color in numerous Protestant denominations share similar frustrations. However, UMC and PC(USA) leaders have greater documentation of women expressing the racially related challenges within their respective denominations. Other predominantly white denominations may have various ways to support clergywomen of color, but they are not promoted in their online resources. Also, the support may be through women's organizations or ethnic caucuses rather than unique resources that address the mutual shaping of inequalities that clergywomen uniquely experience.

6. Although many seek fairness in representation, denominations are slow to understand what constitutes a critical mass for participants versus tokenism, or the proportional percentages necessary to bring about change.

7. See David Kinnaman and Aly Hawkins, *You Lost Me: Why Young Christians Are Leaving Church—and Rethinking Faith* (Grand Rapids, MI: Baker Books, 2011).

1

embracing womanhood

THE STRUGGLE WITH SEXISM

FELICIA DEAS WITH MIHEE KIM-KORT

The greatest trick the devil ever pulled was convincing the world he didn't exist. —KEVIN SPACEY, *THE USUAL SUSPECTS*

Lay 'em down, Sethe. Sword and shield. Down. Down. Both of 'em down. Down by the riverside. Sword and shield. Don't study war no more. Lay all that mess down. —TONI MORRISON, *BELOVED*

~~~~

Growing up, I was taught that the f-word was a dirty word.

Feminism. In some Christian faith communities, it is analogous to communism, to "hippie, make-love-not-war" movements, and to Mother Earth theologies. It is seen as dangerous. It is seen as incompatible with the Bible. It is seen as a threat to the social order and basic community life of the church. And yet, even in those communities that profess to be inclusive and work toward affirming everyone's gifts and callings, especially that of women, we still witness disparities and inequalities. It is more than an issue in terms of income. There remain differences in the numbers of male and female ordained ministers. There remain differences in the number of male pastors of large churches versus female pastors, and like-wise, female pastors of small rural churches—whose numbers are quite high—as opposed to male pastors. There remain differences in expectations, and the number of negative interactions women experience are much more pronounced.

And then, for those who are women of color in this vocation, there is another edge, a double edge to the experience of inequality. Most would agree it is difficult to separate out the struggles of both sexism and racism. While some may say a person's first impression is often shaped by gender before anything else, there is too much—race, class, sexual orientation—that informs these encounters. Yet, something undeniably continues to be present when it comes to the expression of power, especially in such traditional patriarchal communities as Christian churches, and this seems generally universal no matter what the culture. Though stacks and stacks of literature have been written about the topic, modern-day circumstances continue to beg the question: Why do power dynamics, whether race, economics, orientation, but especially of gender, continue to hinder the church from being not only fully representative but also the genuine embodiment of God's kingdom here on earth? Is it simply a matter of Adam versus Eve? —MKK

Women have been in ministry before recorded history. Women have been co-creating with God through childbirth and nurturing and finding ways to keep families and communities together. Yet, when it comes to the formal practice of ministry, women have generally experienced a rocky road. Professional ministry is still primarily a sphere ruled and orchestrated by men. The familiar maxim "The greatest trick the devil ever pulled was convincing the world he did not exist" is applicable because it is the same for the issue of sexism in ministry. To speak of sexism among some groups is to speak to what is generally accepted as a nonexistent problem. The redemptive hopes of a minority always seem to be a vision of peaceful living with the majority where there is acceptance for all. And so, sexism becomes minimized in a quest to pursue greater equality for the larger group.

One of my first assignments as a newly ordained clergywoman was as an administrative assistant to the pastor in the church office. I answered phone calls, put together the Sunday bulletin, organized mailings, and responded to the requests of the pastor. I was dutiful in carrying out my assignments. Although I had had a different vision of my work in the church when I entered seminary, I convinced myself that I was living out my calling in this capacity.

Yet, it was not until I had a casual conversation in the office with a respected male leader of the congregation that I had a moment of clarity. In a celebratory moment, the pastor came in the office with another respected male leader of the church who had recently announced his acceptance in an advanced degree program in religious studies. The pastor patted him adoringly on the back and talked about all the books that would be written by "the one upon whom God had smiled." In the same instant, he turned to me and said, with an equal measure of pride, that I would be the one editing these profound works.

I nodded in agreement and smiled, but I was angry, and in that instant, the idyllic lens through which I looked at life in my community cracked wide open. In that less-than-a-minute exchange, I do not believe I could have felt more invisible. Of the three people who were in that office at that time, two held a master of divinity, and the pastor was not one of them. Yet, I was being relegated to polishing and editing someone else's work instead of being looked at as someone who had the ability to create my own projects and offer them to the world. This seemingly benign incident in a simple church office setting is just one of many pictures of sexism and how it insidiously makes its way even deeper into the pulpits and pews of our church congregations.

CULTURAL WOMANHOOD:
questioning authority in liberation and social movements

People call me a feminist whenever I express sentiments that differentiate me from a door mat or a prostitute. —REBECCA WEST, AUTHOR AND LITERARY CRITIC

I serve in a denomination that was birthed during the civil rights and black power movements of the late 1950s and early 1960s. Our church is so tightly connected with these movements that most people forget that we are first a community of faith. And so, we proudly celebrate Jesus as Black Messiah and honor the notion that God is intricately involved in the liberation struggle of oppressed people throughout the African diaspora. Yet, even as we recognize the oppression of black people in the United States and through-out the diaspora, we continue to struggle with issues of sexism and gender-based oppression.

There is the sense that because we were a church engaged in the liberation struggle of black people in a society where blackness was severely devalued, whatever differences we had among us as men and women would be taken care of within that larger struggle. There was no need to have separate conversations about black wom-anhood and what it meant to be a woman in general or, in particular, an ordained woman of color. In fact, there were some who perceived that these "side conversations" detracted from the greater issue at hand. There was no space to have a meaningful conversation about being branded the editor of the great works of my male colleague without it dissolving into an infuriating conversation about my moods and "what was wrong with me." My gender was sidelined by my culture, and the marginalization I experienced because of it was not seen as legitimate as the issue of race, ethnicity, and culture.

Political commentator and author Melissa V. Harris-Perry, in *Sister Citizen*, advises that "the internal, psychological, emotional, and personal experiences of black women are inherently political because Black women in America have had to continually struggle with negative assumptions about their identity and character."[1] Black women engage in battles regarding our identity and char-acter in all aspects of our lives, including the church. Perhaps, in some cases, it seems that the battles are more evident in the church community because of the difference of power inside and outside the church walls. Black women are expected to be a certain way in wider culture, both by blacks and non-blacks, but within the church the ideal of submission to men continues to be upheld by all, and sometimes it seems even more so by women.

~~~~~

In a similar vein, in many Korean immigrant churches women tra-ditionally do not hold any office, whether as an ordained elder or ordained minister, even within denominations that encourage and even mandate such representation. It certainly was the case in my church. Instinctively, we might assume that the reason is because the men prohibit women from these positions. However, what I had seen and continue to see, in many cases, is that women are equally if not more reluctant to accept the responsibilities of serving on the leadership board. Most expressed that serving in this capacity would invite pressure from an unexpected source, that is, it is greatest from the other women in the congregation. Sometimes there is jealousy or competition. Sometimes there is judgment and anxiety with the disruption of the status quo. Whatever the case, most women would rather not deal with all the added obligations of the leadership roles. Thus, the problem of sexism is not on the radar, or worse yet, avoided and ignored by those it affects most. —MKK

Yet, if you asked any leaders or members of the congregation about sexism in the church, most would respond promptly and then insist that it does not exist, and certainly not in the church. This declaration of denial usually appeared in my church congregation in the tagline "anybody can be in leadership if they want to be." This was taken to mean that anyone with proper capability and initiative could assume a place among the church leaders to make decisions and affect the flow of worship and shape the members of the congregation. In fact, there was some truth in this declaration, because as you looked out among the congregation, there were indeed a greater number of ordained clergywomen than you would find in most churches. However, the number of ordained women in a congregation is no better indicator to the practice of sexism than the number of black friends one has is to the proclivity one has to be racist. These are not reliable indicators. We could not look out at the numbers of female ministers and proclaim there were no gender-specific issues that we needed to address as a congregation.

One of the greatest challenges to shedding light on sexism in the church is getting people to acknowledge it and then talk frankly and respectfully about it. It is difficult to call it out without feeling a sense of betrayal to the liberation struggle of black people and the black men with whom you work and respect and those who even influenced your calling and journey. Even as I write, I am keenly aware of the desire to minimize and explain away some of the behavior and attitudes of my male colleagues because I know they are not bad people. That is a continuous conflict within myself. I have learned, though, that sexist and misogynist ideas are not held only by bad people. Very well-intentioned and loving people have the ability to hold traditional ideas about the roles men and women are supposed to hold in society and in the church. When it comes to ordination the process is not always so straightforward or black-and-white.

In my denomination, there is not a formal ordination process where there are different boards or committees. For a long time, ordination was conferred based on the work one did for the church—teaching, work with the children, community service. I was part of a second generation of ministers who attended seminary and obtained a master of divinity degree. When the church governing body announced that there would be an ordination ceremony, no one would know whose name would be called during the service. I remember being in the final year of seminary and being in church when the announcement was made calling for the following brothers and sisters to come forward for the laying on of hands. I figured that since I was in my last year of seminary, my name would be called out as well, as I had seen with others, and especially my male counterparts. It was not. I was devastated.

CHRISTIAN WOMANHOOD:
self-proclamation as power and authority

> I would like to be known as an intelligent woman, a courageous woman, a loving woman, a woman who teaches by being.
> —Maya Angelou

After that experience, I had to get clear with myself about what ministry meant for me and about whether I would continue my work with or without the title of "Reverend" before my name. So, having made my peace, I finished school, I gave birth to my son, and then I found myself in church and hearing another announcement about ordination. Except this time I did not bother to get excited. In fact, I began to nurse my son in the back of the sanctuary, readying myself to congratulate the person whose name was announced to the congregation. Of course, my name was called, and immediately I had to cover and put myself back together, and after I handed my son to an usher, I walked up before the congregation.

In some regards, I did not become aware of gender issues on a personal level until that day when I became an ordained minister. As I look back on it now, I think it was significant, even portentous, that I was nursing my firstborn child when I was called before the congregation to participate in the rite of ordination and the laying on of hands. It proved to be a rather meaningful foreshadowing of some of the struggles I would continue to encounter in this season.

I have come to conclude that part of the difficulty with addressing sexism in the church is twofold. On one hand, it is difficult to reconcile that the house of God, the last place of refuge for those who have been cast aside by the larger society, is an imperfect place run by imperfect people. It has long been traditionally held, yet largely unspoken, that the pastor in the black church is not only the leader of the church but also the representative of God on earth. There is something in the walk of the traditionally male pastor that sets him apart and makes him a human of a different order.

On the other hand, acknowledging sexism in the congregation means that we must take action against it. We must do something, right? This is the place where most of us get stuck. As a young and newly ordained member of the congregation I found myself engaged in battles that ironically put me face to face with other women in the congregation who felt that I did not represent the ministry as it ought to be represented in the pulpit. Most of the things at issue were not about roles or responsibilities. It was not about guiding me to discernment about how I would minister to people and lead programs, but rather about the possibility that I might broach topics like the tendency to centralize power with the pastor that questioned the congregation's quasi-idolatrous relationship to the pastor and the worship experience itself. If any concern was offered it was a question about how I dressed on a Sunday morning. People expressed concern about my standing before the congregation with bare legs and opened-toed shoes. People showed concern about the possibility of tears in the pulpit.

One colleague shares her struggle with the receiving line at the end of a worship service, which was often the time when the parishioners would comment on everything from her hairstyle to whether she was loud enough in the pulpit. She also explains the various nicknames she obtained from congregation members, particularly from an older male. An Asian American clergywoman, she tells that he loved to call her "Doll" and even explained to her one day that she reminded him of a beautiful porcelain doll. Other nicknames or "terms of endearment" can range from "angel" to "kid." While our male clergy counterparts may have to endure undesirable sentiments about their haircut or facial hair, it is a rare occurrence for them to receive such blatantly sexist comments. These experiences mark clergywomen and not only marginalize them but also have a way of demeaning the office of the ministry and invalidating the position and authority of women ministers. Some clergywomen struggle with how much these perceptions shape their own understanding of their own ministry, their capabilities, and their gifts. —MKK

For me, a favorite example of female pastoral leadership comes from the fictional character Baby Suggs in Toni Morrison's *Beloved*.[2] Baby Suggs was a former slave who, after suffering the tragedies of chattel slavery—watching her children sold and having her body broken—lives out her life of freedom as an "unchurched preacher." Her home is the heart of the community, and she offers a space where people can begin to experience their humanity again after being regarded as property for so long. I admired the fact that she did not need the formality of an ordination or the drama of a call story in order to serve the people of her community. Her ministry emanated from her very being. She had the ability to speak to the needs of the people who came to her door seeking food, shelter, comfort, messages from loved ones, and even grace. I could think of few better images that exemplified Jesus' own ministry, where his work was rooted in his identity and not by some outside human authority. He loved and served the people, and that was that.

Likewise, it was the model of Baby Suggs as this broken woman who offered her heart to a broken community that served as a vision of pastoral leadership to me during those times when I felt that I could no longer navigate the tightrope of ordained ministry within the church setting. As much as seminary prepared me to put together well-constructed sermons, to exegete texts, and to experience myself as pastor in different learning contexts, it could not have prepared me for assumptions about my ability to lead or serve based on open-toed shoes or bare legs or a less-than-perfect religious journey. It takes much discernment and strength to not take it personally when, after preaching a sermon you are asked, "Is everything okay?" or "What is going on with you?" as if every passionate delivery is indicative of a stress-induced tirade rather than my merely making space for the Holy Spirit to allow me to be transparent and honest before the congregation.

STRATEGIC FEMINISM:
discovering the power of radical submission

It was not until I was ready to leave my calling and ministry behind that I found my pastoral identity and began to lead from my own sense of authority. I feel that God has placed a call on my heart to lead people and to offer them grace and freedom from the self-imposed limitations that prevent them from experiencing the fullness of life. And while I feel fully empowered as a woman, my identity and my sense of authority are not rooted solely in my gender. When the pressure of molding myself into the congregation's vision of what my leadership should look like and the unspoken expectation that I needed to dim certain aspects of my feminine self became too much for me to bear, I had to offer that grace to myself and receive it from myself, as one who has authority.

At the same time, I had to be willing to lose it all—the expectations, the standards, the blueprints for ministry. The call on my life was not given to me by any ordination board, ministerial panel, or pastoral search committee. It was not placed within me at birth by the usher board, the elders, or the pastor. I recognize and accept that whether I am called "Reverend" or "Miss," I hold that call in my own heart and hands in whatever context I may find myself.

Still, there is an intricate dance between fighting the invisible enemy and learning when to embrace that which I despise about this journey. For women of color who engage in ministry, the choice to embrace womanhood is a revolutionary choice. Embracing it is subversive and powerful. Embracing womanhood is the choice to open your heart to relationships with other women. Embracing womanhood is to look into the face of oppression and open your heart to it—not in a "hate the sin, love the sinner" way, but to know that oppression does not have the power to snuff out your ability to co-create with God and to work to build God's kingdom on earth. Embracing womanhood is not simply embracing a label of biblical equality and feminism but a revolutionary love that was first exemplified by Jesus' empowering and inviting ministry toward all.

~~~~~~

I had to stop fighting. The chip on my shoulder had become an enormous boulder, sometimes one that felt the size of this planet. The comments, the interactions, the expectations overshadowed everything, and soon it seemed nothing was positive or good about not only ministry but also the church universal. I felt the anger had turned into bitterness, a bitterness that began to seep into my ministry. It seeped into my faith life. It seeped into my relationship with God. At some point the anger—the righteous anger of the Old Testament prophets, the one that shatters barriers and glass ceilings, walls and rose-colored glasses, doors and windows where I felt like an outsider with my face pressed up onto the glass desperate to be let in—settled into resentment and had lost efficacy. It became useless in my journey, and so I had to find another way. —ANONYMOUS CLERGYWOMAN

~~~~~~

I discovered a strategy, one that has helped me to survive on some days and flourish in others. *There is a time to fight, and then there is a time to embrace.* It is a delicate balance, a dance of sorts. If you behave as though gender-role oppression does not exist, then you do a disservice to your congregation and to yourself, and to all the women who struggle in this cause. There are times when the ills are so deeply rooted and solutions are hard to come by; however, the simple act of seeing what is there becomes freeing and healing. Many suffer in silence because of the unconscious conspiracy to act as though the problem is nonexistent. Yet, at the same time, our consciousness about the problem cannot be so keyed in that we are constantly at battle with others about it.

There comes a time when we must consider the merit of surrender and trusting that God will make it right, and so we lay it down—the sword and shield, the fights about stockings and open-toed shoes, the belief that clergywomen must be aesthetically muted and sexless, and the idea that the greatest role for ordained clergy-women is as best supporting actress. Laying it down does not admit defeat or loss. But it has meant for me a radical trust in a God who will use us in ways that are beyond our best plans, our highest educational pursuits, and our most courageous ambitions. Sometimes surrender, and laying it down, is the best strategy after all. Who better to demonstrate that to me than Jesus Christ, and is that not enough? And so, I hear him say to me, again and again, "Lay it down. Sister, lay it down."

> Our strategy should be to lay siege to empire with our ability to tell our own stories. Stories that are different from the ones we're being brainwashed to believe. The corporate revolution will collapse if we refuse to buy what they are selling—their ideas, their version of history, their wars, their weapons. Remember this: We be many and they be few. Another world is not only possible, she is on her way. On a quiet day, I can hear her breathing. —ARUNDHATI ROY, AUTHOR AND ACTIVIST

Notes

1. Melissa V. Harris-Perry, *Sister Citizen: Shame, Stereotypes, and Black Women in America* (New Haven, CT: Yale University Press, 2011), 5.
2. Toni Morrison, *Beloved* (New York: Penguin Putnam, 1998), 87.

2

where are you *really* from?

THE STRUGGLE WITH RACISM

YANA J. PAGAN AND RUTH-AIMÉE BELONNI-ROSARIO
WITH MIHEE KIM-KORT

If I were really asked to define myself, I wouldn't start with race; I wouldn't start with blackness; I wouldn't start with gender; I wouldn't start with feminism. I would start with stripping down to what fundamentally informs my life, which is that I'm a seeker on the path. I think of feminism, and I think of antiracist struggles as part of it. But where I stand spiritually is, steadfastly, on a path about love. —BELL HOOKS, AUTHOR AND SOCIAL CRITIC

What are you?

I see that inquiring look in people's eyes when they first meet me. In the context of ministry, it is often the lead question: Where are you from? Let me guess. China/Japan/Korea? Are you Puerto Rican/Dominican/Mexican? African? Whether I am offering pastoral care in my office or at someone's home or even if I run into someone who somehow knows me through someone else, "How long have you been in this country?" is often a default question. When it quickly disintegrates into a guessing game, I can only reroute the questions to the person after an affirming smile and a "Good job for guessing correctly!"

18

This point of introduction happens frequently, and I wonder how much of it is out of a social awkwardness—as in, "I can't come up with anything else to say right now"—or the pressure to categorize a person in order to feel safe and make myself, the other, more familiar, less foreign. I always got the sense that it had little to do with genuinely wanting to know me. It seemed like asking a superficial question where the answer might confirm the assumption in the other person's mind was the goal and then the other person could move on. Rarely did it ever seem like a genuine interest in wanting to know about my family, my traditions, or my ethnic culture.

Who are you?

The issue of race persists in the experience of young clergywomen of color. Along with gender, it is usually a source of discomfort and unease, especially in the context of ministry when the expectations are for white, older males, or at the very least, white females. Sometimes the way to manage these predicaments is by avoiding these issues or to move to the other extreme by being on the defensive. In a society that continues to perpetuate these issues and even purports to be color-blind, the impetus has to begin with us, those in the middle, those entrenched in these questions, and those who can speak conscientiously and critically about how these issues are important to address and navigate particularly in the context of the church. It requires an honest and persistent endeavor to reflect on the various ways racism is enmeshed in the church's language and theology, and our personal histories with the effect of racism on our experience of faith. —MKK

SEEING RACE: playing the part

YANA J. PAGAN

I do not recall having ever experienced racism with the Hispanic community even coming from a church with Puerto Ricans, Dominicans, Venezuelans, and Mexicans within the same community. It is sad for me to admit, but my encounter with racism has always been in places that were different from my cultural context.

I remember being asked to speak in an interview where the discussion was on racism as a sin for an e-magazine called *Ethics Daily*. It was there I became aware of how few people are willing to discuss this issue. People hesitated and avoided the word and often diluted and whitewashed situations. Although I was proud of *Ethics Daily* for taking the initiative for this project, I was disappointed and dismayed that so many people were afraid to admit that they have some racist perspectives. Christians seem quick to say that they are not racist, but if, as a second-generation Puerto Rican, I enter their church on a Sunday morning, I'm looked at with condescension or caution, as a child or as a hot wire zone, someone who should be avoided by all.

I truly believe that we are all made in the image of God, and the existence of racism makes me angry because I know it grieves my heavenly Parent because we are equally precious in God's sight. Often it isn't the overt expressions of racism but the subtle and passive-aggressive racism that causes a rise out of me. For example, members of a church I attended for some time constantly commented on my Spanish accent even though English is my first language. Or when people have the inability to "place me" because of my light complexion, so they incessantly ask, "What are you?"

I was definitely angry about such experiences in the beginning.

At this point I'm not irate about racism all the time because I've learned to play the part. In a way, it's a coping mechanism, it helps me to survive, but I see it as dangerous ground that women tread when the issues become too much to address each day. I know that when I am invited to preach it is important for me to ask about the environment. What is culturally acceptable? What is appropriate? What is a hindrance? What is helpful?

Still, the persistence of racist culture has made me defensive. I have to work not to be offended or offensive, but I also have to be on my guard. I have long, wild curls, and it takes a lot of courage to let my hair down—literally. I can't help but wonder if even my hair would deter people from hearing me preach God's word. I want people to take me seriously, so I have the tendency to make sure my hair is neatly pulled back. This may seem like an insignificant sacrifice to someone else, but it has changed my ministerial identity because I have understood that to be respected in particular circles you have to play the part. Even as a Latina in the year 2013, when we have a black president in the United States, I still have to do my hair a certain way and dress the part to be heard and seen as a person, much less a pastor.

ACKNOWLEDGING RACE: DEFINING AND CREATING COMMUNITY

I remember in seminary becoming aware that so many women were struggling with their call to ministry because they were in churches that would never allow them to be ordained leaders. Furthermore, women who were not Anglo-Saxon shared how we had to deal with more prejudice toward our identity and ministry. I did the only thing I knew how to do based on the wisdom from my pastor from New York City, Rev. Raphael Martell, and the associate pastor, Rev. Dr. Loida Martell. I created something. I started a group called Blended Women in Ministry. "Blended" because no matter what race we were, we had in common a call to ministry, but we were all women who face the consequences of racism.

Using Scripture in relevant ways, I tried to encourage these women to press forward. One of the most important pieces was making sure that the women who entered the group signed a covenant so that our group could be a safe place. I wanted this to be a place where we could share anything, including the difficult struggles during internships where we were treated differently because of the color of our skin. There was no one skin color that experienced more or less racism. Racism is racism. Whether someone says something indirectly or directly prejudiced about my culture, it is racist. Even if it isn't physically violent, it is emotionally and spiritually violent. Sometimes the worst experiences within the church are not the way a person might look or speak to me but the way that we would interact with each other.

That Blended Women in Ministry group has taught me the importance of relationship. Relationships allow us to have conversations and to feel safe to be intimate about our thoughts and lives. Racism is the antithesis of relationship because its assumptions and prejudices prevent you from being in dialogue with the other, but when you are in relationship with the other, conversations unfold. Therefore it was the wisdom of my favorite passage of Scripture that led me to glean from the boldness of the woman at the well. John 4:9-10 (THE MESSAGE) says, "The Samaritan woman, taken aback, asked, 'How come you, a Jew, are asking me, a Samaritan woman, for a drink?' (Jews in those days wouldn't be caught dead talking to Samaritans.) Jesus answered, 'If you knew the generosity of God and who I am, you would be asking *me* for a drink, and I would give you fresh, living water.'"

The Samaritan woman was honest, and because of her courage she is changed forever. Even in their brief encounter, she and Jesus engaged in honest dialogue. Jesus was not afraid of her because she was from Samaria, and she was not afraid of him because he was a Jew. Although Jesus had the power to draw water for himself, he asked her for a cup of water. It was this shared need that initiated a brief theological conversation absent of judgments that otherwise might have been part of their interaction. In that absence I believe that both left the well blessed by each other's presence even though they were from two different worlds. This was a glimmering of God's kingdom reconciled and realized in relationship—and it opened the door to reconcile an entire community to Christ.

EMBRACING RACE:
planting my feet in other worlds

RUTH-AIMÉE BELONNI-ROSARIO

The struggle is inner: Chicano, indio, American Indian, mojado, mexicano, immigrant Latino, Anglo in power, working class Anglo, Black, Asian—our psyches resemble the bordertowns and are populated by the same people. The struggle has always been inner, and is played out in outer terrains. Awareness of our situation must come before inner changes, which in turn come before changes in society. Nothing happens in the "real" world unless it first happens in the images in our heads. —GLORIA E. ANZALDÚA, *BORDERLANDS/LA FRONTERA: THE NEW MESTIZA*

I am dual.

I am Afro-Caribbean. I have Martinican as well as Puerto Rican heritage. My father was born and raised in Martinique. His native language is French. Because of his ability to speak multiple languages, he moved to Puerto Rico and settled when he met and married my mother. My mother is a native of Puerto Rico. She is the youngest daughter of a black, divorced port worker and of the white daughter of well-to-do small business owners. Both of my parents speak Spanish, French, and English. I lived in a house where my father spoke to us in Spanish with a French accent, because my parents decided that it was best for us to learn English as a second language. Being proficient in English was seen as a symbol of progress and opportunity; French was connected to his perception of Martinican poverty.

I grew up in a house where my white grandmother, then a widow, took care of us. Taking us everywhere she went, she was congratulated often on her good deed of taking care of four of us "black unfortunate children." This attitude toward us, her grandchildren, upset her greatly, to the point of putting people in their place by educating them about our family composition and the need to stop these racist comments. I also lived in a house where the economic status of my family was torn by the existent racism toward black immigrants from the Caribbean to Puerto Rico. This prevented my father from having access to "honorable" jobs, ultimately leading my parents to an impending divorce. This is a small portrait of where I come from: an interracial and intercultural marriage. My parents were proud to be Martinican and Puerto Rican, but they wanted their children to be better as the "American" label demanded and dictated to us.

Knowing my story and acknowledging both what is beautiful and difficult added so much to my ability to minister. But it is something I endure and challenge to varying degrees knowing that the issues of race, as I experience it and as my sister colleagues experience it, persist and manifest themselves in many ways. I am faithful to this process because I believe God calls me to it, not only vocationally but personally. In a way, it feels as though Jesus Christ laid the path for us in the way he sprawls across the human and divine while seeking to be inclusive of all of humanity, calling anyone to join him in the work of redemption.

mmm

In ministry, this straddling of both worlds frequently felt confusing. My father liked to remind me that as soon as I stepped foot through our front door we were entering his country, and because of blood, our country: "Out there you are in America; here you speak our language, eat your mother's food, and live in the place where your parents were born." In the beginning it was difficult to reconcile the clashing worlds, most notably when it came to working, living, and being, whether in the church or not. And then, I began to see this experience as an asset. Who among us does not have to experience more than one culture, whether it is race or geography, economics or gender? The more I embraced this part of my identity, the more I felt I could minister to a wide range of people, and not only understand them but also have compassion and love for them. Because they were not strangers to me. They were family because they were God's children, too. —**MKK**

mmm

QUESTIONING RACE: IT IS BLACK AND WHITE

> Change is the one unavoidable, irresistible, ongoing reality of the universe. To us, that makes it the most powerful reality, and just another word for God. —OCTAVIA E. BUTLER, *PARABLE OF THE SOWER*

Much has changed for me since my time in seminary to my present situation where I work and minister on a daily basis in different venues. The change was not always easy, but now I see it as a necessity for growth. Taking a seminary class on theories of race now after years in ministry has given me eyes to see these concepts and structures in new ways. When it came to experiences of racism, I saw the ways these theories held up, and at the same time how sometimes they felt impractical when applied in the real world.

My current and continuous encounter with racism is not only in discriminatory comments from ignorant people around me or prejudice and stereotypes inflicted on me by larger society. In fact, two fundamental experiences that have influenced my understanding of racism and persist in my need to constantly engage these issues come from much larger phenomena—colonialism and religion. Yet, even though these are separate movements in and of themselves, these two enormous instruments of human construction are difficult to tease out and separate from each other. The colonialism in my parents' countries' histories were complicated and intertwined with religious agendas but also political and economic pursuits. The intentions of missionaries may have seemed spiritual and benign, but they were fraught with much more, as history would reveal to us.

And so, as a result of this history and my experience in the United States, I find myself having to fight against my own colonized mind every day and differentiate my personal religious experience from its institutionalized understanding and teachings, particularly in the negative by-products associated with colonialism. I see the need to continue to define racism: to call it out, to name it, and to challenge it in tangible ways.

First, I define racism, coming out of these experiences, as a matter of control and domination. It is so deeply embedded in the way we think and perceive others that we might not be conscious of it. When a friend tells me that she cannot help but cross over to the other side of the street when a black man is walking down the street toward her and she is alone, I see that this thinking is indicative of racist structures. We are conditioned to treat and interact with people in a certain way, in a prescribed manner. This forges a way for people to cultivate their suspicions toward others, particularly others of different races. It is a matter of inflicting a diminishing, helpless complex on one's self based on skin color and then forcing one to believe it to be true while one is struggling with feelings of helplessness. This idea is also perpetrated by the institution of religion and its missionary conquests to the Caribbean. Religion's misinterpretation and distortion of theological teachings by priests, friars, and other religious leaders during the time of colonization and conquest, and even to our day, have shaped the deeply rooted understanding that whites are good, noble, and Christ-like people, and in turn all that is non-white is intrinsically opposite.

The binary perspective that has come out of and shapes black versus white permeates much even within the church, within the language of faith, and within the practical exercise of ministry. What

it can often look like is a hierarchy of values and preferables. The hierarchy becomes a rigid structure where certain things are liked or upheld more—anything from worship songs to liturgy to mission projects to styles of preaching—and often passed off as tradition or even orthodox. This system becomes engrained in the culture and can be internalized in unintentional ways by those who are on the margins, even if they are in leadership positions. I often angrily lamented the ways I was complicit in these oppressive structures by silencing my own voice because I felt that to speak would disrupt the comfortable and familiar status quo. Those moments where I felt the Holy Spirit urging me to speak often went ignored out of fear or anxiety that if I did or said anything to invalidate the more prevalent experience of the dominant culture, somehow I would invalidate myself. And I did this not only to my detriment but also to the detriment of the wider cause of Christ and God's kingdom.
—ANONYMOUS CLERGYWOMAN

Consequently, I see I am a product of this back-and-forth struggle and this interplay. Colonialism is ever-present in my formation, as the two countries that influenced me are, to this day, imperial endeavors of the United States of America (Puerto Rico) and France (Martinique). And while religion has undeniably been a part of this colonialism, it is nevertheless key to my faith formation and current placement in professional life. I am a product of church education and ordained ministry. In reflecting on who I am and how far I have come—being displaced in another country in the metropolis of New York City—in light of the readings and teachings in my seminary education, I found myself questioning some aspects of my life. They are not easy questions, and the answers so far are even less desirable.

This is why I now feel in my bones, in my flesh and blood, that my whole life has been a lie. All I thought was good and well-deserved appears not to be in light of what I have discovered about the insidious nature of colonialistic and oppressive tendencies in my religious upbringing. The lie about "work hard and you will make it," the old Reformed Protestant (later called American) work ethic, has become apparent in the interplay of these two experiences. Racism for me is someone or some group designating who one is, and making an intentional decision that affects who I am and making me believe it, making me hate myself for it, and making me feel less of a person and social contributor. At the same time, the designators seem to expect thanks for their help (the so-called help and vision to civilize and teach the right way to the other, the stranger) when I have accomplished a goal, assuming my achievement was because of their help.

After reading texts, listening to lectures, and having class discussions, I see the mix of races in my family with suspicion. I come from a diverse family where intercultural and biracial marriages are the order of the day. Before this family portrait, I questioned, Why? What were their intentions? Why did they choose to go against the social status quo? Were they ever in danger? Was it worth it? Was there ever love? Was skin color so determinative when it came to who was worthy of love? Why did they choose this path of life? Why did they choose it for us? Where is God in all of this?

I feel these questions I ask are legitimate, and at the same time, I feel conditioned to ask them. It is a conundrum that I see myself confront over and over. Am I legitimate, authentic, or conditioned? There are plenty of examples of interracial and interethnic marriages in Scripture; there are plenty of examples on how to treat the stranger and the other with love, compassion, and a welcoming attitude. But colonizers, along with their religious leaders and missional intentions, distorted and reshuffled their teachings to accommodate their imperialist agenda. Thus, I find myself at a crossroads: legitimacy versus imposition. How do I reconcile having in mind that by me going through this search I am proving the systematized power of racism?

Willie Jennings writes, "We have a distorted view of theology. We have distorted the message of intimacy intended by God in the person of Christ Jesus."[1] For that reason I am haunted by more questions and uncertainties: Do I want to work hard? For what? Where do I want to go? I feel all my goals have been set before me and set for me. I feel I did not have any saying in the decision making on the course of my life. I feel stripped, tricked, and short-changed. I feel naked while at the same time clothed with new lenses. Race is a lie, an illusion.

And so, I further define racism as an intentional and premeditated invention on the part of the group in power. Racism is based on an illusion that makes one believe one has determining power over another. We can see how throughout the history of colonization, racism has been essential in the development of the capitalist world. All this stems from a white supremacist society whose founding is based in an ideology of the inherent superiority of white Europeans over non-whites, an ideology that was used to justify the crimes against indigenous people and Africans that created the nation.[2]

CONFRONTING RACISM: NEW PERSPECTIVE AND SHATTERING THE ILLUSIONS

I continue to define racism by describing it as an illusion that keeps one trapped while at the same time giving one the illusory freedom to go to any place. I have always thought I have been privileged or lucky. I have been able to overcome some hurdles of racism, but the reality is that not everyone can say the same. Even with what I have accomplished for my own life, I know there were people in power who decided favorably on my behalf. This illusory freedom makes one think that all of one's accomplishments are a result of working hard while dismissing the fact that, in achieving those accomplishments, one has been blinded and directed in behaving a certain way, and specifically in a way dictated by people in power. This is a reality that I was confronted with when I migrated to the United States because of the clear and palpable American racial binary framework.

Having a binary perspective, and a dual narrative, of black and white makes one lose focus of the greater picture. "Black" has been used to denigrate every human being who is not white Anglo-Saxon (or Iberian, or Germanic). The interesting thing with having so many immigrants arriving each day is that it threatens the white supremacist narrative and structure of the country. What white supremacy is doing is continuing the white/black binary. It is the old yet effective divide-and-conquer strategy. You keep white, and some type of whiteness, as desirable and norm. If you make light-skinned immigrants think they can pass as white, then your divide-and-conquer strategy becomes even more powerful and more detrimental to the majority of the population.

I am learning to seek out contradictions. These contradictions are no longer a source of unease and disquiet in the negative sense. They disrupt the status quo that often blinds us to the realities that need God's radical redemption. Those contradictions help me to see through the illusions and speak to a larger vision of God's kingdom. The binaries I encounter—when I honestly delve into them by engaging and deconstructing them—end up becoming the most fruitful instruments of dismantling the wider systems of race.
—ANONYMOUS CLERGYWOMAN

Ultimately, racism is an illusion that keeps one trapped while at the same time giving one a false sense of freedom to go anywhere. How does one combat an illusion if all that one sees, and even more fundamentally, all that one imagines, dreams, and created, is conditioned by this pervasive illusion? In some ways, racism, in my opinion, as experienced by the oppressed, is then living in ignorance of the space and time one (as a non-white person) has been conditioned to live in, and feeling affirmed about where one has gone, and then true freedom and liberation is having one's eyes opened to the truth, to the systematized way of doing things and how they are determined by the dominant culture.

Confronted by this reality, empowered by my righteous disgust, I feel passionately about the work to bring it down, to dismantle it, that innocuous feeling "great" about one's accomplishments based on the oppression of standards set by someone else. In doing so, I see the need to continue advocating, empowering, and encouraging others to do so, while advocating to avoid any resurgence in the future. I am well aware I, by myself, cannot change or abolish racism. But I strongly believe (it might be interpreted as naïvité) that as an individual I will not allow "white" to define me, to hate me, or to condition me. I do not want my context of having a double colonized heritage dictate who I think of myself when I look in the mirror. I will put those assumptions aside. I don't want to be a Beke[3] or ever become one.

After reflecting on the anatomy of racism as influenced by my story, I ask myself the ultimate question: Should I view all that is in my life as truly legitimate? Should I feel that I have truly lived my life authentically? Should I feel proud and content with myself, my accomplishments, and where have I arrived, despite realizing that my life has been conditioned by the dominant culture, those powers and principalities? I have to respond that despite all that I have discovered and felt especially in recent seasons, that the hope of Christ drives me to say a resounding yes. My story may have been one that has been conditioned by negative structures of religious colonialism, but by the same familiar composition a kernel of the gospel has taken root and risen above the soil, and it is growing and giving me the power and spirit to work to abolish what is in opposition to God's true kingdom. I have been empowered to seek ways to terminate it, to make partnerships with other racial-ethnic groups and give voice to their concerns and plight.

Above all, I find myself being and wanting to be subversive about this anatomy of racism by echoing Aimé Césaire's words:[4] *Ninguna raza tiene monopolio de belleza, inteligencia o fuerza,*[5] as well as appropriating the words of Jensen: "Race is a fiction we must never accept. Race is a fact we must never forget."[6] Despite the embedded racism, I affirm Césaire's view of *el negro: Negritud es la afirmación de que uno es negro y orgulloso de serlo.*[7] After reflecting on my family history and heritage, seeing it in light of various readings, lectures, conversations, and my own articulations, I find myself no longer diminished but empowered to let the world know that I am "negra" and as such I am extraordinary, I have much to offer, and I am proud to be so. It is not always black and white, but when I am able to speak to the black and white, those racist structures, I see that I have caused a chink and crack in those structures, and I am helping to make space for God's kingdom to truly break through into our realities.

Notes

1. Willie James Jennings, *The Christian Imagination* (New Haven, CT: Yale University Press, 2010), 57.
2. Robert Jensen, *The Heart of Whiteness: Confronting Race, Racism, and White Privilege* (San Francisco: City Lights Publishers, 2005), 4.
3. El Beke is a state of mind where the *criollo blanco* hates *el negro*, *el mulato* dreams of being *blanco*, and *el negro* dreams of *mejorar la raza* (bettering the race). This definition is found in Eugenio Fernández Méndez, *Crónicas de las poblaciones*

negras en el Caribe francés (San Juan: Centro de Estudios Avanzados de Puerto Rico y el Caribe, 2008), 64.

4. Césaire was a Martinican poet who spoke against the cultural and psychological alienation of *el negro* in Martinique, a poet who fought against the colonialist state of mind that still haunts Martinique.

5. Roughly translated: No race has a monopoly on beauty, intelligence, and strength. Méndez, *Crónicas de las poblaciones negras en el Caribe francés*, 67.

6. Jensen, *Heart of Whiteness*, 14.

7. Roughly translated: Blackness is the affirmation that one is black and proud to be so. Méndez, *Crónicas de las poblaciones negras en el Caribe francés*, 64.

3

you're *how* old?

THE STRUGGLE WITH AGEISM

MIHEE KIM-KORT WITH LeQUITA HOPGOOD PORTER

Age isn't how old you are but how old you feel. —GABRIEL GAR-CÍA MÁRQUEZ, WINNER OF THE NOBEL PRIZE FOR LITERATURE

Let no one despise your youth, but set the believers an example in speech and conduct, in love, in faith, in purity. —1 TIMOTHY 4:12 (NRSV)

Age is not always a state of mind.

The adage is useful only in certain situations, and it is not straightforward depending on the situation or community. As far as I am concerned, people have a much more profound influence on one's state of mind than I care to admit to myself. It is why, for as long as I can remember, I have struggled with how I might be perceived by others—as a woman, as a woman of color, and especially as a young woman of color. I can come up with any number of stories about serving in ministry, and particularly in youth ministry, where I easily blended in with the high school students if we were out together at a game or a movie or a restaurant for dinner. I endured nicknames and endearments like "kid" from parents and other congregation members because I was "just one of the [youth]." Before going into ministry, while I earned a meager living as a substitute teacher fresh out of college, I was often mistaken for a high school student, even a middle school student. I was stopped in the hallways between classes by other staff who asked sternly, "Where are you supposed to be now?"

Where are you supposed to be now?

That would be a question that would haunt me day in and day out as I wrestled with so many different aspects of my identity early on in ministry. Not only the question *where?* but also *what?* and *who?* On the one hand, I thought that it would be a boon to seem like one of the youth—fresh, relevant, and exciting to be around— while still being respectable and an authority figure. On the other hand, I felt that my shifting from one context to another, whether working with youth or facilitating an older-adult Bible study, whether teaching elementary-aged children on Sunday morning or attending a board meeting on Tuesday evening—confused not only the people around me but also myself. It was a challenge trying to navigate people's assumptions about me based on my age, and then to work out exactly what and how I felt about ministry and my passions and interests. In more ways than one I would short-change myself, lower the bar, and downplay my authority or experience because I felt that my age automatically discounted it. I did not want to explain or justify myself. It felt easier to say: *I'm young. I'm green. I'm wet behind the ears. I'm a newbie.*

But there is the other side of the coin: It is not only perceived youth that burdens or detracts from one's abilities. Even those who are seasoned in life, those with more than a few gray hairs and lines worn into their faces, also encounter a layer of prejudice. As always there are exceptions to every case, so these generalizations are helpful only insofar as they do not detract from the necessary and potentially helpful conversations about age, generation, and ministry. Nevertheless, the frequent presumption with an older generation is that they are entrenched in their opinions and have a narrow, limited perspective, a one-sided opinion about everything. The older generation is seen as "not with it," and at a certain point, even irrelevant and ineffective in ministry because they seem unable to connect with a younger generation or contemporary culture. And so, my good friend Rev. LeQuita Hopgood Porter and I offer our reflections on the struggle with both in the context of age discrimination, and a dialogue about what it means to encounter not only frustrating limitations and restrictions but also full-out judgment of who we are based on the year we happened to be born into the world.

> Most people don't grow up. Most people age. They find parking spaces, honor their credit cards, get married, have children, and call that maturity. What that is, is aging. —MAYA ANGELOU, AUTHOR AND POET

> Women may be the one group that grows more radical with age. —GLORIA STEINEM, AUTHOR AND ACTIVIST

THE ELDERLY:
becoming older or being open?

LeQUITA HOPGOOD PORTER

Age is more than a number. It shapes our community relationships; it informs one-on-one interactions, and, for better or worse, it is a way of categorizing people. In some cultures, age is valued, and in others, it is a disadvantage. In my experience, I have encountered a wide range of perspectives on the value of age. Ageism, as I understand it, is discrimination against a person based on her or his age. In Asia, Africa, the Caribbean, and other societies, elders are respected, held in high esteem, and valued for their wisdom and experience, while youth are seen as those who "should be seen and not heard." In contrast, generally our society does not respect the elderly, and the wider culture, as seen in pop culture and other media, idolizes and glorifies youth for their energy and openness. In either case, an unspoken hierarchy exists that privileges one over the other based on an arbitrary number—years of life.

Even more so, I saw this same disconnect within the church. During seminary, I learned from classmates of different denominations that even in churches there is clearly a glass ceiling for women in ministry starting at the age of fifty. I had not expected to encounter any kind of ceiling for those who are called into ministry.

Being a member of the Baptist tradition, I was not aware of any set limitations—because if a woman could get in at all, her age did not matter. In my culture and denomination, it was truly amazing if a woman was received as a minister in the first place.

Between my years of practice as a minister and my experience with ministers as a young woman growing up in the church, age was an important factor when it came to church leadership. A minister was older and therefore seasoned and experienced, and quite frankly, *he* always represented a sort of father figure—someone who would give good advice in a loving way and tell you everything you needed to know about this distant God. Sometimes, the minister even represented God in so many ways. While many churches seemed to value the middle-aged pastor with a young family as ideal, the minister was clearly an authority figure, and more likely, the older, the better. Sometimes it was not always so consistent or clear-cut, but for the most part, age was always associated with wisdom and authority.

I never personally knew any ministers, but ours were always men whom we listened to on Sundays and did not bother any other times of the week. I remember one of our ministers, Rev. White, who was a great teacher and disciplinarian. He taught us the Bible, but he also was intentional about teaching the adults of the church about church protocol. He was also intentional about the children learning how to participate in church activities and would make us take opportunities to learn Scripture and recite prayers. It did not matter if we were afraid or extremely nervous; he would direct us to pray and would wait until we finished crying in order to hear the words come out of our mouths. At the time, we thought this was cruel, but I can say in hindsight that he caused us to push beyond the fear and to learn how to speak up in church services, and how to be a part of the worship. Other than Rev. White, I have few memories of our ministers growing up—and I have attended church regularly all of my life. Pastors/ministers were often distant, and only occasionally, when I heard the adults talking about something the pastor had done, would I learn something that let me know the minister was not someone I wanted to know personally.

Another minister I remember from my childhood was in his forties when he became pastor of our church; I was a teenager. Although he did not seem as aloof as the others, there was still a clear divide between the young people and the pastor. He was and is superb at pastoral care—prayer and visitation of the sick—and I witnessed him excel in those areas. But he was not a highly educated man, and to be honest, at the time I did not feel I could learn much from him—but was I ever wrong! Again, I learned in hindsight, a lot from witnessing his extreme care and stability in the face of grief and despair. I learned that even though I never sat with him and had a conversation about what he did as a pastor. I learned from his walk what it meant to be a pastor who cares and who is available to minister to the people, even those who may have been against him and caused him much despair. He talked the talk, but he also walked the walk. Even though he did not believe in the validity of women preachers, he was very supportive of my educational pursuits and successes, and so good to my parents until the day each of them passed away. For that personal care and concern alone, I will always be indebted to him.

These were not the only experiences that shaped my understanding of calling and ministry. I had a more positive interaction with someone in the church, someone who looked past my age and gender and saw me as a whole human being, and therefore, someone who could and had received God's blessing to become a minister. It would be a moment that would shape my sense of calling and identity as a minister.

I was interning in Jamaica during my seminary days, and an elder deacon, who was eighty-three years of age, needed counsel regarding a difficult issue in his life. At the moment he began to share and open up his area of pain, I thought to myself, "My God, this man could be my dad . . . Lord, whatever am I going to tell him?" I was much younger than he—forty-three years old—but at the end of the session, he thanked me and told me that he didn't believe that a woman could ever counsel him on anything spiritual, and *especially* a woman so much younger, but that he had learned differently that day.

While the deacon was surprised by the experience, I was much more surprised by it. Age dissolved in the midst of the Holy Spirit connecting us to each other based on our faithfulness and openness in the moment, and the blessings were abundant for both of us. At that instant, my view of being a minister shifted dramatically, and I began to mature in my understanding of God's call on anybody's life—at *any* age. What mattered more was the honest and gracious relationship building that happened in this situation.

> The call of God is not just for a select few but for everyone. Whether I hear God's call or not depends on the condition of my ears, and exactly what I hear depends upon my spiritual attitude. —OSWALD CHAMBERS, *MY UTMOST FOR HIS HIGHEST*

I had accepted a call to the preaching ministry later in life, the ripe age of forty-two. I say it was ripe, because I felt in my prime. I was at my peak—mentally, physically, psychologically, emotionally, and intellectually. I had practiced law and worked in business for many years, and now I was embarking on the most exciting adventure of my life. I embraced my life journey, and I saw that I had so much to glean from my experiences as resources. I was confident in myself and rooted in my own identity. Nothing could deter me from this new season of life. When I accepted my call to preach and pursue ordained ministry, my pastor, Dr. J. Michael Sanders of New Jersey, said two important words to me that will stick with me forever: "No limits!"

No limits.

I would not let anything or anyone be a limitation to me, especially if others based those limitations on stereotypes or the expectations of the world—or the church. God had given me so much in my life all these years, and I saw that there was nothing out of God's reach in my life. Nothing was impossible for God, and God was with me, so I believed my pastor's words. And so, I would do my best and never expect anything less of myself.

Still, it was not always easy. I found opposition and conflict in the most unexpected places. One of the first obstacles I encountered was the rejection of women ministers, young and old, in general. I'm still unsure of the cause—whether competition over scarcity of available pastorates, or even insecurities as we all tried to navigate these waters. There were no blatant attacks at first, but there was enough innuendo to let me know that I was not welcome in a field that was dominated by men. I often think how devastating this would have been had I experienced this at a younger age. By the time I accepted my call I had already slain some dragons and trampled some demons in my thinking about myself, so this apparent rejection served only to fuel me to do better and go higher. I wonder if my age and experience gave me the strength to press on because I had already encountered so much. I was more determined than ever to answer God's call, and only God could put a stop to my ministry.

Ultimately, I believe my age (years alive), acquired level of maturity, experience with people, resolve to pursue and complete a task—God used all this in my favor. I was married, so I received a level of respect that I do not think I would have gotten had I been single. I was already a mother raising children, so I got some extra points for the added responsibility of having a family. Most of all, in my flesh and blood, in the very marrow of my bones, I was bound to this calling, so the easy attacks could not gain any traction with me, and I believe that others could see this commitment. I was focused—I was on a mission for God.

What was the root of my focus? I eventually embraced every bit of learning I received in my early years as part of my education—shaping, molding, and preparing—to lead me in God's calling. Even to this present day, all of that is thoroughly utilized to fulfill my call.

The benefit of dealing with people over all these years has strengthened my ability to navigate the minefield which oftentimes is the church. The stereotypes and expectations, the agendas and hierarchies will always exist, whether within or outside the church walls. I have come full circle to see that age truly is a state of mind, when one intends it. I tell myself and others: *Age alone does not qualify or disqualify anyone for anything.* Age can also be advantageous, and truly useful, even when it may not seem like it to others. Regardless, what is immensely more important is the skill a person gains in the special experiences of life, which can uniquely equip someone to lead others effectively for God's purpose. All this cultivates a new kind of openness that embraces so many possibilities because I have encountered so many possibilities already, an openness that, ironically, I would never have discovered in my youth. Every life experience has a potential teaching moment, and the more life experiences, the better.

> As you grow older, you will discover that you have two hands.
> One for helping yourself, the other for helping others.
> —AUDREY HEPBURN, ACTRESS AND HUMANITARIAN

I am known for a saying at our church: *"Don't let this gray hair fool you, I'm just getting started!"* And I mean it. While some may be thinking retirement, I am thinking, *"Lord, what's next?"* I am more excited about the opportunities ahead than I have ever been about those behind me because I know God can and will use whomever God chooses to fulfill God's divine plan. The Lord will equip me for the work at hand, whatever my age. God is faithful to me, and I will continue to be faithful in the pursuit of these adventures especially in the future! I am a firm believer that, as my father told me years ago, it will always be my faith, hope, the Holy Spirit, and holding onto God's unchanging hand that are the keys to doing anything good for God.

> Youth is happy because it has the capacity to see beauty. Anyone who keeps the ability to see beauty never grows old. —FRANZ KAFKA, NOVELIST

THE YOUNG: clueless or courageous?

MIHEE KIM-KORT

> It takes a very long time to become young. —PABLO PICASSO, ARTIST

> No [one] is an island, entire of itself; every[one] is a piece of the continent, a part of the main. If a clod be washed away by the sea, Europe is the less, as well as if a promontory were, as well as if a manor of thy friend's or of thine own were: any [one's] death diminishes me, because I am involved in [human]kind, and therefore never send to know for whom the bells tolls; it tolls for thee. —JOHN DONNE, "NO MAN IS AN ISLAND"

Clueless.

It was a movie loosely based on Jane Austen's *Emma*, starring Alicia Silverstone and Paul Rudd, about a superficial high school teenager whose life is effortless and uncomplicated until she attempts to meddle in her friends' lives—only to find it all backfires.

The story comes to a head when the Emma character is forced to confront what she really wants in life, and therefore, how completely *clueless* she has been all along. While not the best rendition of such a literary classic, it is truly a classic of my generation and brings back some nostalgic moments about the 1990s, adolescence, and discovering one's identity.

Even now, *clueless* would be a word to describe me at times. I do not mean this in a self-deprecating or pejorative sense. I will be the first to admit that I have not always been aware of certain things in a head-in-the-clouds kind of way. Growing up I was a bit naïve, idealistic, and always assumed the best in others. It took a long while to discover that not everyone wanted to be nice or helpful, and even more so that most people looked out for themselves, first and foremost. And then, even the church was not utopia. It was *not* a community of people who perfectly loved each other, where all people were considered equally, and judgment and prejudice were absent.

> Remember, you cannot be both young and wise. Young people who pretend to be wise to the ways of the world are mostly just cynics. Cynicism masquerades as wisdom, but it is the farthest thing from it. Because cynics don't learn anything. Because cynicism is a self-imposed blindness, a rejection of the world because we are afraid it will hurt us or disappoint us. Cynics always say no. But saying "yes" begins things. Saying "yes" is how things grow. Saying "yes" leads to knowledge. "Yes" is for young people. So for as long as you have the strength to, say "yes." —STEPHEN COLBERT, POLITICAL SATIRIST AND ACTOR

I became cynical. With age I became jaded and disillusioned about people, their motives, their agendas, and their pursuits. And so, somehow I really believed and thought this was growing up.

When I finished seminary and got my degree, my ordination certificate, and my first calling, I regained some of that innocence from my youth. I entered my first ministry wide-eyed and hopeful, my mind and heart overflowing with all that I had learned in seminary, both in the classroom and outside of it, lofty words and ideas about church, kingdom, and redemption. I could barely contain my excitement at sharing what I believed would be revolutionary and transforming to my church community in ways that I imagined would later be described as "life-changing" and "miraculous."

My first call was as an associate pastor for youth and Christian education. I remember so many of the first comments I received were reactions about my youthfulness.

"Oh, you are so young!"

"Why, you're just one of the kids!"

"You could be my daughter/granddaughter/child!"

As someone who grew up with the constant reminder not to rock the boat, I never responded honestly. I remembered all that I was taught during my childhood growing up in a traditional Korean faith community. As children and young people, we were told repeatedly that respect for our elders meant silence and obedience. When an elder or deacon approached us, it was always required that we bow deeply and call them by their proper title according to the church community. If we did not show this respect, it was akin to committing some kind of sin. Likewise, any dissent, conflict, or opposition meant that we were being rebellious toward God. Ironically, I have hardly heard of an immigrant Korean church community that has not split off into smaller churches because of some kind of power struggle and confrontation.

At this point in my new ministry, I desperately needed to legitimize my position. I wanted to say something about my years of experiences with churches and young people, and how I had passed my ordination exams in one try. I wanted to explain how I had a high GPA when I graduated from seminary, and even earned a fellowship for a senior thesis. I wanted to tell them about how I had driven across the country by myself a few times for an internship in Colorado and had seen and experienced much in my travels. Instead, I would awkwardly say, "Thank you," or "I know," all with a smile and maybe even a slight blush, as if it were a compliment, so somehow the appropriate response meant I should look cute and grateful. But deep down inside I knew something was off. I eventually internalized these expectations. I looked young to people so, yes, I must be young. And that meant, well, clueless.

But there were some advantages to embracing this perception. When I made any mistakes, people were much more forgiving. *Oh, she's just starting out,* or *She's just learning how to do it.* In so

many ways, I felt I had opportunities to experiment and try anything when it came to ministry. Moreover, I felt that the children
and youth gravitated toward me a little more; after all, I almost
looked like one of them. I was fun. I was energetic. I was silly. I
was a more attractive and engaging representation of the church
than the gray-hairs sitting in the pews or teaching Sunday school.
Finally, it seemed like I had the energy to do much more, even if I
felt exhausted after a long weekend retreat or an all-nighter lock-in.
I convinced myself I had the fortitude to do it all, and much more.

And yet, I realized that as much as I *could* minister in this way, I
found that ultimately I was selling myself short. I was selling God's
calling for me short. I was selling short, too, the importance of
God's ministry in whatever sphere, to whatever demographic. I
allowed myself to conform to others' false perceptions of myself,
rather than God's expectations for my life, my ministry. I found
myself becoming a bit crestfallen about my identity in ministry. I
had assumed that my degree and ordination would automatically
make me into a respected authority figure. Instead, I found myself
back on square one, struggling with the same obstacles I did as an
actual young person—people who thought I was incapable, inex-
perienced, immature, and ignorant. And even worse, I started to
wonder if this was possibly true.

I turned a corner during my second call as an associate pastor
for youth and children. I began to hear the same first impressions
again. Except this time, I said, "Yes," and ignored the comments.
I laughed at them and forced myself to forget them, and then I
focused on what was really important. Granted, this method did
not always work, and my husband can certainly attest to the many
times I went home complaining about one incident or another when
I was mistaken for a youth group member.

But this time I made a deliberate effort to not internalize these
comments and instead proclaim reminders to myself of my calling
in Jesus Christ. Sometimes that proclamation we are called to as
ministers of the word and sacrament are not just for the congregation but for ourselves. I needed to preach to myself about God's
grace and redemption just as much as I needed to preach to the
congregation on Sunday mornings.

And then, I discovered that my youth was an asset, and not just
in terms of getting away with some mistakes, or being a draw to

youth, or having energy for silly weekends. I started to see the ways our culture only seemed to worship youth and younger generations by paying homage through constant images of youth in advertisements, movies, sports, and much more. In reality, however, our youth were experiencing marginalization and oppression in enormous ways. Finally, I saw that my youthfulness could be a way to identify with and stand in solidarity with a demographic that was experiencing pressure from so many sides. This was something I understood in my own bones.

This generated a new kind of thinking for me in ministry. I recalled that the most influential theologies I read in seminary were liberation theologies. It led me to approach this ministry with a liberative theological posture toward youth. I thought about black theologies and feminist theologies, even the Asian American feminist theology that was formulating in my own mind, and all these were helpful in the way I approached youth, interacted with youth, and cared for and encouraged the youth in my community. When I remembered the ways I had been limited within my church community not only as a young person or a young woman but also as a young woman in an Asian culture, I could see the various ways, both subtle and blatant, that youth are often limited by their communities. And so I wanted to offer a space and ministry that would liberate youth from these bindings in order to fully embrace God's love, acceptance, and calling to them.

Most importantly, I wanted to instill in youth the value and power of relationships rooted in a God who seeks to liberate us. It was only in communities that made space for authentic stories that a profoundly redemptive perspective could transform not only relationships but also identities. It was in community that I discovered the courage to step out and be fully me, no matter what the expectation or assumption. I could hardly think of a better attitude to pass on to youth in my church communities: To find the courage to embrace what God is doing in one's life no matter what the season and to speak, live, and love boldly from it.

I learned about this from the youth in my churches over and over again.

4

finding your place

THE STRUGGLE WITH COMMUNITY

LAURA MARIKO CHEIFETZ

We have all known the long loneliness and we have learned that the only solution is love and that love comes with community. —Dorothy Day, journalist and activist

I alone cannot change the world, but I can cast a stone across the waters to create many ripples. —Mother Teresa, winner of the Nobel Peace Prize

No one is without culture.

Every person has a cultural background, shaped by race, class, region, schools attended, nationality, generation, gender identity, sexual orientation, and any other number of shaping factors. Women of color in ministry, particularly those in white dominant denominations, are likely to serve in a ministry context with a culture that varies significantly from their own or from the context in which they were formed as people of faith. That is, women of color are minoritized.[1] Other minority statuses, such as being from another region or country, being single, being LGBQ or transgender,[2] or being childfree[3] can further differentiate the clergywoman from those with whom she ministers.

Each ministry setting has its own specific culture. While every new minister entering that ministry has to learn the context, women of color whose own background differs by race and class (and thereby culture) face additional challenges to connecting with community members and, perhaps, additional opportunities to bring a fresh perspective to that ministry.

In this chapter, I will rely on the use of all kinds of categories. I do not believe all these categories are real. For example, I believe race is a social construct meant to allocate power and privilege to white people. However, I believe these categories have real consequences for our society, our identities, the ways in which our political process functions, and our access to resources.

TESTIMONY:
faith journey in community

The most common way people give up their power is by thinking they don't have any. —ALICE WALKER, POET AND NOVELIST

I am *hapa yonsei*. I am a multiracial Asian American, fourth-generation Japanese American on my mother's side. My father is white, of Jewish descent. We are thoroughly Presbyterian; my father converted to Christianity in college, and my mother grew up at First Presbyterian Church in Berkeley, California. The three of us are Presbyterian ministers. My younger brother is an artist, and I credit him with keeping us in touch with what I call normal.

Growing up, the space where I could be the most myself was in my home. Our particular racial and cultural fusion was normal to me. We developed our cultural identities at home. When I was a young teenager, my mother decided we needed to practice the Friday night Shabbat meal together as a family. My Japanese American Presbyterian mother engaged us in practice of an aspect of the culture of my Jewish Presbyterian father, who was raised on more political rallies than Shabbat services.

Outside of our home, I learned I was not normative according to the racial and cultural milieu surrounding us. I grew up in mostly white communities and in white secular Pacific Northwest churches. My pastors were always white. My teachers were white. Elected officials were white. When others encountered me or my family, it was all too common to be greeted with a sense that we were not normal. "That's so *interesting*!" people said when they knew my background, and "What are you?" when they didn't. I felt different, but never excluded beyond the occasional racial slur. Being in church with other Asian Americans and multiracial people happened only occasionally. My dad once preached about racism and told a story in the sermon about an experience my mother, brother, and I had; this was the only time my reality as a person of color was addressed in church in my growing-up years.

When I was looking for a call, the form Presbyterians fill out had a question that said, "Are you willing to serve in a church or institution composed mainly of persons of another race/ethnicity other than your own?" The question always made me laugh. What if I said no?

Enter my first call: leadership development and vocational discernment with Asian Pacific American young adults and pastors. Imagine this fourth-generation multiracial person interacting with a wildly diverse group of people, most of whom were second-generation from Asian Pacific American churches. We were all lumped into the same racial category of Asian American, we shared experiences of racism, we were all Christians, but we did not all share the same culture.[4]

In my second position, also a ministry position outside of the parish context, I worked with an intergenerational multiracial constituency. I was always secretly worried I would get pigeon-holed into ministry only with people of color or with young adults given my limited work experience and my status as a person of color (and as a young adult until recently). I was excited to work with some white people, too. I quickly realized that the constituencies with which I had to acquaint myself were largely east-of-the-Mississippi groups of highly educated people, many with a higher class background than my own, or at least many of whom grew up with higher-income parents, and dominated by white people and black people. I had also moved to the Deep South, an area that is far more Christian in its culture.

I have yet to engage in ministry in a cultural milieu that is congruent with my own.

COMMUNITY:
the interaction between culture and faith

Culture is complicated, to say the least. I use "culture" as defined by lifeways, language, and worldview.[5] These three aspects of culture might be seen as layers, with lifeways at the surface level. Lifeways, or traditions and practices, are the most visible and easily identified. Language and worldview represent progressively less visible yet more foundational layers of culture.

LIFEWAYS

The topmost level of culture, the parts we can all see, are lifeways. Lifeways are affirming and necessary to cultural identity. It is important to me that I know to send *koden*[6] when a family member dies, a practice informed by my Japanese heritage. Courtesy of my Jewish roots, I feel free to get grumpy with God and approach the Scriptures with both respect and suspicion.[7]

Lifeways are accessible aspects of culture because they are prone to consumption. I have learned what to order at a Korean restaurant, which is helpful considering so many of my colleagues in ministry and so many fellow Christians are Korean and Korean American. I have learned about the roots of hip-hop, which some worshipping communities are claiming as a faith expression.[8]

I served a multicultural church in a full-time internship during seminary, in which my lack of maturity, my inability to negotiate properly the cultural differences between us, and the church's challenges caught up with all of us. I worked in San Francisco at an urban church that was the result of a merger between a majority white congregation and a majority Latino congregation. My own need for a division between us, and some semblance of keeping working hours below sixty per week, clashed significantly with the customs of the church and its pastor. From the immigrant members of the church, I learned that being an immigrant in the United States is a 24/7 job, with its attendant complications of negotiating between generations in the same family, language, cultural differences, laws, and the high cost of living in the Bay Area. I had become progressively more vegetarian between the ages of fourteen and twenty-four; this church and its members ate meat, so in order to participate in the life of the church I became a functional omnivore. And I did eat my fair share of meat: shredded beef tacos, chicken soup, turkey sandwiches. I participated in rituals of celebration and of food. I was able to consume these lifeways, but this learning was inadequate to understand the culture of the people with whom I ministered.

It is one thing to know if the community would prefer that you bring a casserole for a potluck as opposed to bringing artisan bread and a bottle of wine. It is altogether different to assume knowing which is right will suffice as a way to know and understand the ministry context. Being in ministry is more than knowing these little aspects of culture. For the people with whom the clergywoman ministers, this is also insufficient. They may know you can speak about your Korean grandmother and her cooking during your sermon, but if that is where their knowledge ends, they do not truly know you.

Lifeways can also be described as window dressing. Relying on lifeways as a way of understanding or connecting with a ministry context is insufficient.

LANGUAGE

Language is the next deepest layer of culture. Language gives our words possibility and practice. A clergywoman colleague stated that she uses her mother tongue when referring to family members in front of church members, who are majority white. She told me, "When I'm talking about Papi, I say 'Papi.' I don't say 'Dad.'" And yet, language is more than speaking Spanish in liturgy or doing a language study of a word from your mother tongue in your sermon to make a point. It shapes our understandings of what the world is like, and who we might be.[9]

Language is not limited to those of us who speak the language of our ancestors. I do not speak Japanese or Yiddish or Russian or Polish, but I have a language that shapes my thinking. I am thoroughly urban, definitely late Generation X. I can be straightforward, even loud. But when interacting with older people or when visiting another country, I revert to what I call Japanese American. I use cautious, deferential language. In this mode, I squeeze myself into the smallest amount of space possible. Once my 1.5-generation[10] Korean American supervisor told me, annoyed, "Don't do that thing . . . where you apologize for existing."

At the multicultural church where I served in my internship, I scrambled to learn the language; my training had neglected to teach me Californian Spanglish or the proper metaphors to help me better minister to Latinos. Sometimes when I preached in Spanish, I could tell my metaphors were completely off. Even if I was technically intelligible, I wasn't making sense. What would an indigenous person who speaks at least three languages, serving as a line cook and raising kids in San Francisco, care about *The Matrix*?

By the time I spent a summer preaching at a Taiwanese church of immigrants and their children, I had found a way to connect. I could use my knowledge of immigration policy in the state of Georgia and the United States and my experience being friends with 1.5- and second-generation Asian Americans and Latinos, and balance that with an understanding of what a fairly well-educated group of professionals would be able to hear. My metaphors appeared to make more sense. My dislike of immigration policy wrought by states upon their population during the first term of President Barack Obama was something that could connect with the story of Moses, with the kind of ministry Jesus did, and with this congregation.

And still, we did not completely understand each other.

WORLDVIEW

The deepest layer of culture is worldview. It is how a group of people sees the world, what people believe about the world. Worldview is about interpretation. This is shaped by history, geography, and the myths we tell of our origin and life together. The dominant cultural worldview in the United States is that this is the greatest country in the world. This is a particularly strong narrative that shapes our discourse and our foreign policy. It has yet to be tempered by facts that the United States lags behind other nations in literacy, achievement in math and science, human rights, paid family leave, and numerous health measures, yet has a higher rate of incarceration for black men than apartheid South Africa.[11] Another aspect of this dominant worldview is the belief that Christianity is central to our DNA as the best country. This civil religion is often lived out in our churches and ministries, despite the fact that we as Christians belong to an international faith.

I hold to beliefs that run counter to this worldview. As someone experiencing the United States as a minoritized person, I find I approach life, ministry, and witness as a Christian much differently. I have preached the protest that the biblical text brings to the reality experienced by poor people, women, and people of color, or to those countries occupied by the United States. As the guest preacher, I can get away with quite a lot. But for those who serve in a congregation long-term, these words are not always welcome. Even in my ministry in educational organizations, I sometimes feel like the broken record in the room. If the United States is the greatest country in the world, then why must we continue to hold up the realities of those who struggle to be treated as human beings each day? Why do our experiences often contradict this narrative? One Asian American pastor told me that her experiences as a woman of color made her acutely aware of the dynamics of race and class in the context of the church's ministries. She said,

> I realized that the realities that I faced on a daily basis were choices for [my white parishioners] to talk about or not. So maybe they would talk about racism and gun violence today or maybe they will just focus on gun violence without examining systemic racism and oppressive systems in our city that could contribute to it. The complexities that I am aware of, some of which I face on a daily basis, just weren't on their radars in the same way.

MINISTRY: integrating faith, culture, and community in creative ways

Pull up a chair. Take a taste. Come join us. Life is so endlessly delicious. —RUTH REICHL

Being called to ministry is a gift. In ministry, we bring our souls to the work before us, and people bring their lives and beings to us. We don't do it for the money. We do it for the reign of God. We do it for the people of God. We do it because it is our most natural response to the gift of faith.

Fundamentally, we are all human: clergy and church people alike. We all experience joy and suffering. Ministry is not wholly an us–them activity. At its best, it is a we activity (coupled with healthy self-differentiation). In reality, minoritized clergywomen may feel even more keenly the differences between ourselves and the people we are called to serve because ministry calls us to work so closely with others in our community.

A Latina minister I interviewed for this chapter came to parish ministry reluctantly. She felt her call was ministry with immigrants. She discovered that members of her wealthy and mostly white community opened up to other cultures through music, so early on in her tenure at the church, she sang the Prayer of Illumination in English and Spanish. People were moved, referring to it for months afterward. Ultimately, she says, even if she were to serve a church less open to multiple languages and practices, she will always find a way to celebrate her culture through her ministry.

One Asian American minister described her approach in working in a white urban church context as one in which she brought up difference in conversations and meetings over and over, and ultimately she decided it would be easier to avoid those discussions when possible because they had become too hurtful. She felt the members and other leaders of the church were very defensive, although the young adults were the most likely to be receptive to conversations about particularities of context and the impact on their faith. It became an exhausting and alienating experience to encourage the congregation to think about issues of diversity and racism.

She changed her approach. She found if she could address the topic of difference without using any racial or ethnic labels, she could get further in the conversation with white church members. She states:

> As their pastor, I tried consistently to meet them where they were, utilize my own identity as a starting point in the conversation, and try to push them to deeper realities. I had to

consistently expose myself to vulnerabilities to educate them. Sadly, I don't feel as though they got it many times.

To be honest, I enjoy immersing myself in places. I do not always feel like a stranger. I like to ferret out cultural quirks and claim a place as my own. I treat the communities I serve the same way I treat places. I want to find the community member who has a particular piece of the community's history to tell, the same way I want to find the best local bakery or café. I want to identify the major players in a community and then turn around to look for those who are often faithful community members but are ignored, the same way I want to find out are the major concerns regarding food insecurity or homelessness in any new community. I want to figure out alternative paths the way I want to walk around an unfamiliar neighborhood and scope out the interesting gardens or tiny side streets.

I believe it is possible to find oneself at home in one's call. In each place and space I have engaged in ministry, I have been embraced. I share the values and the commitments of those spaces. I formed relationships that have been transforming. I do not believe that feeling out of place is inevitable for those of us who find ourselves ministering across divides of race, culture, ideology, sexual orientation, or family structure. But I have experienced in each place jarring moments that remind me of my difference.

Questions I ask myself are: How do I bridge the gap? And is this a one-way project? Working by myself to bridge the gap can be exhausting. Imagine stretching yourself across a span and waving your hands looking for the hands of those on the other side. Now imagine those hands aren't there. That won't work forever.

Nadia Bolz-Weber uses the phrase "culturally commute" to refer to what the people in the congregation she serves have to do to attend traditional church. Women of color serving in a context that does not reflect our realities have to culturally commute between home and social life, and often between our heart language and the life and language of the place we serve. For the Asian American clergywoman I interviewed, she found it easier to do the work of commuting, meeting the members of the community where they were, rather than expect them to meet her where she is. I have found I tend to try to adapt to the culture of the place, forgetting the very real ways in which I contribute to creating that culture, until I find myself panicking that I am losing myself, dissolving into that culture.

Discussing the very real ways in which one person's life is different from another's at an individual and systemic level is a genuine way to ask others to work to bridge the gap with us. This has the potential to lead to a good bit of sanity. Our realities as women of color are just as real as the realities of the places and people we serve. The Latina minister I interviewed found herself in a conversation with a parishioner who believed undocumented immigrants were taking jobs away from U.S. citizens. She countered that person's arguments with research and personal experience, humanizing the issue and educating the parishioner. She also taught that person about the gap between realities: the parishioner's perceived reality of what was true about the job market and undocumented immigrants, and her experiences of the actual, lived realities of undocumented people and what the raw numbers indicate undocumented immigrants do for employment.

CODE-SWITCHING:
the language of fluid ministry and community

When I came to my second call—national ecumenical work where I was the first person on staff who was neither black nor white—my white middle-aged supervisor called me into her office and asked why I act so differently in different situations. "I'm code-switching," I said. "But I'm not being fake. All of this is part of who I am." I explained I learned this as a multiracial person, particularly as one navigating the national black-white racial construction. As a multiracial person, I know how to navigate life with various racial groups. I learned this as someone "not Asian enough," because I didn't grow up in Asian American churches. As a queer woman, I know how to operate within communities who would find my identity and my primary relationship anathema to their beliefs. As a Generation X-er, I know how to interact appropriately with Baby Boomers.

Sometimes I wish I could just hang out with people like me. But ministry was never meant to be that way. Ministry is not a social club. Most of us are not called to minister to sameness. We are called to be a part of communities not our own. We are called to care for these people, to live God's love for them. We are called to share ourselves with them. And if we are honest, many of our parishioners culturally commute to church, too. We are not the only ones set apart culturally. Our race or ethnicity or regional background may make us different, but many parishioners enter a church world that does not resemble their work world. Even with increasing diversity in our social circles and our work worlds, and even with some interesting minor changes in the racial make-up of churches, the majority of US churches remain overwhelmingly monoracial.[12] Some parishioners who leave their neighborhoods to attend church commute between the cultures of where they live and where they worship.

After living my life in churches and communities that look nothing like me, I am usually comfortable with not being part of a church or a wider church ministry that reflects my racial and cultural realities. I move a lot, and having grown up a pastors' kid, I have come to expect the complications of getting to know new places and spaces. In my ministry, I am always different from those I serve in one way or another. The Scriptures are rife with contexts in which cultural, religious, and ethnic differences define relationships or provide opportunities to challenge the divisions those differences create. Paul often waded into communities of believers wrestling with these differences.

What my particular experience in church gives me is a leg up in ministry. I have an edge in that I expect my ministry settings to be significantly different from that to which I am accustomed. From what I have heard from friends and colleagues who serve in ministry, they too have to navigate the cultural differences within each ministry context, even if they share a common racial background. Ministry is often a constant cross-cultural exercise, with each ministry setting having a unique culture shaped by its history and identity. I also spend a great deal of energy navigating those differences and attempting to find common ground with those with whom I am in ministry. I find myself going through phases where I insert my cultural reality into conversations because it is a way of making space for my whole self.

Being aware of the shaping power of my own cultural upbringing is important to being in ministry with people who don't share my culture. Sometimes I do something very Japanese, like refuse something I really want. Japanese Americans are taught it is polite to refuse a gift or offered refreshments multiple times before reluctantly accepting. When I catch myself at this, I laugh and explain to my colleague or friend, who is usually confused at my refusal. In turn, I have had to train myself not to be offended when someone immediately accepts the proffered gift or takes the last piece of pie instead of offering it to everyone before taking it.

I grew up where religion was almost anathema, with parents who explained to us as children that we wouldn't send Christmas cards to all our friends and family because so many people in our circle were not Christian. Now, living in a place steeped in Christian religiosity, I am training myself to see this place on its own merits, instead of simply looking down on the South as insensitive to diverse religious traditions.

Doing this work of ministry requires that we take the people and the places we serve seriously. Ministry in the twenty-first century means we do not use our ministry settings to meet our own social, spiritual, sexual, or relational needs. Our ministry settings are not for us. If we seek to have our ministry settings meet our own needs, we have a larger problem than cultural differences. We have any number of other places to meet our needs. We can, as a private individual, particularly those of us in urban areas, go to gatherings of our communities. We can visit home. We can keep in touch with our friends. We can read and watch what feeds our souls. This, of course, is far less available to those of us in small towns and rural areas. I can't imagine what the postmaster in the small town where I spent the first eight years of my life would have done with my *bitch* magazine or *Heeb: The New Jew Review*.

The role of minister is not to change the space to meet one's own needs. But the role of a minister may be to point to the necessary changes for the full flourishing of the humanity of all. This may mean having some of those difficult conversations with the people we serve, and it may mean leaving and looking for a place that accepts our full humanity. It may also mean learning to open up our own hearts to embrace the wholeness of the place where we engage in ministry, with all its quirks and particularities. We might be called to a community that is not our own and possibly even foreign to us, even as we might be seen as foreigners. And yet, I have no doubt that God uses clergywomen of color to embody the redefinition of community and how that might be lived out in fuller and richer ways.

Notes

1. Within the United States, non-dominant groups are made into theoretical and cultural minorities by the power majority. See the use of the term in *Decolonizing Epistemologies: Latina/o Theology and Philosophy,* Ada María Isasi-Díaz and Eduardo Mendieta, eds. (Bronx, NY: Fordham University Press, 2012), 3.

2. LGBQ signifies lesbian, gay, bisexual, and queer or questioning. I list transgender separately because it is a gender identity, not a sexual orientation. "Queer" was historically used as a negative epithet but has been embraced by many as an umbrella term, more inclusive than "gay" or "lesbian."

3. This term is a positive alternative to "childless," which assumes a household with children is normative, while households without children are somehow socially deviant. I was first introduced to this term by the blogosphere. The use of this term does not, however, necessarily indicate a permanent status or a negative orientation toward children.

4. Viji Nakka-Cammauf and Timothy Tseng, eds., *Asian American Christianity: A Reader* (San Francisco, CA: Institute for the Study of Asian American Christianity, August 2009); Pyong Gap Min and Jung Ha Kim, eds., *Religions in Asian America: Building Faith Communities* (Lanham, MD: AltaMira Press, 2001); Russell Jeung, *New Asian American Churches: The Religious Construction of Race* (New Brunswick, NJ: Rutgers University Press, 2004).

5. Framework from Robette Dias, executive director of Crossroads Antiracism and Organizing, from Dr. Luanna Ross, professor at the University of Washington.

6. *Koden* is a monetary contribution in honor of the person who has died, practiced in Japanese American culture.

7. Talking back at God is considered part of Jewish identity. See Joanne Plank, "Arguing with God Is Part of Jewish Faith, Says Rabbi," *The Seattle Times,* June 16, 1990.

8. The first hip-hop I saw in a Christian context was while attending youth church at the Faith Apostolic Church in Chicago. I have been following the career of former classmate and artist Gilead7 (http://www.myspace.com/gilead7) and the career of J. Kwest (http://www.jkwest.com/), an artist, activist, and pastor in Chicago.

9. There is a plethora of research on this topic. Robin Lakoff's *The Language War* (Berkeley, CA: University of California Press, 2000) explores how language is about power and jump-started some of my own thinking on the subject. A helpful example of cognitive research on the power of language is referenced in Lera Boroditsky, "Lost in Translation," *The Wall Street Journal,* July 23, 2010, http://online.wsj.com/article/SB10001424052748703467304575383131592767868.html (accessed August 21, 2013). Jessica Gross wrote a blog for TED entitled "Five Examples of How the Languages We Speak Can Affect the Way We Think," http://blog.ted.com/2013/02/19/5-examples-of-how-the-languages-we-speak-can-affect-the-way-we-think/ posted February 19, 2013 (accessed August 21, 2013).

10. Mary Yu Danico, "The 1.5 Generation: Becoming Korean American in Hawaii," and Ana Lucia Gonzalez, "Hispanics in the U.S.: A New Generation" (http://www.bbc.co.uk/news/10209099), along with other scholars and cultural critics, have identified a generation between first-generation immigrants (those who arrived in the United States as adults) and second-generation immigrants (those born in the United States to first-generation immigrants or those who arrived very young). Thus, 1.5-generation immigrants are those who arrive as children, after spending significant growing-up time in their countries of origin.

11. The United States has the highest rate of incarceration in the world for all citizens. African American men are most disproportionately incarcerated.

12. Mark Chaves, *American Religion: Contemporary Trends* (Princeton, NJ: Princeton University Press, 2011), 31.

5

we need you

THE STRUGGLE WITH TOKENISM

MIHEE KIM-KORT

Tokenism does not change stereotypes of social systems but works to preserve them, since it dulls the revolutionary impulse. —MARY DALY, RADICAL FEMINIST PHILOSOPHER AND THEOLOGIAN

I am the only one.

On most committees or organizations, I am usually the only one. The only woman. The only young person. The only racial "minority." The only liberal. And most recently, the only mother with young children. It was something I grew accustomed to rather quickly, this being the *token* fill-in-the-blank.

Growing up in suburban, white neighborhoods and attending equally homogenous schools, I was used to being different. Some days I enjoyed being distinct from others. I loved seeing friends experience Korean cuisine for the first time when they came over to my house, or their interest and delight when I managed to supply a few Korean words upon request for translation of any English word, or when they met my "cute" parents (because they were so tiny and novel).

Of course, later I would see how incredibly offensive all of this was, not only to me but also to my family. My parents hated hearing that my friends thought they were "cute," as though they were toys. Sometimes being the only one, or being different, was a way for those with any power or agency to keep those like me strangely dependent on them, whether for affirmation or validation. It took me a long time to see this power dynamic. Even though my parents would tell me over and over, "Be different," I started to see this as confusing and mostly negative advice.

But being the only one has its advantages, too. Sometimes being the only one means more resources. Sometimes being the only one means being a spokesperson and having a monopoly on a discussion. Sometimes being the only one means people look to you automatically to be the embodiment or giver of insight into something specific.

My denomination has something called the Committee on Representation, which at various levels works to ensure an equitable representation (according to clergy and layperson, race, gender) in all the groups and bodies within the church. This includes everything from the local church governing board to committees at the national church level. I had never given it much thought until a close friend and colleague shared some of her experience chairing the committee in her geographical area. She joked that it was an "easy gig," that meetings were usually held by phone or email, and that the bulk of the work mostly required vocal accountability.

There is a strange tension. On the one hand, it is wonderful that there exists a structure that is intentional about helping us maintain a level playing field when it comes to voices, and more importantly, votes. I think such a level playing field is not only an institutional necessity for decision making and development but also an institutional expression of power and agency. Because we have been entrenched in inequalities for so long, it makes sense to have a plan where this is addressed over and over until it becomes a part of our social consciousness—so that in the future, we will not need a committee to help us with diversity. No doubt, it remains imperative that we continue to raise awareness about inequities and privilege, and to be a voice for the voiceless, and to close the gap between those on the center and on the periphery.

On the other hand, there is a tendency toward tokenism in such efforts. The easy gig, meaning, the easily dismissible task that is so easy it can be done over the phone or through periodic email exchanges, of any committee on representation means that we look for the surface qualities of people, as if these were what we want present in these leadership groups. It is sometimes a soft solution to our discomfort with these inequalities.

Yet, there is clearly a backlash to institutionalizing cultural diversity. In my ministry journey, I have worked in both Anglo and Korean churches, and in both communities, there are always huge differences based on both race and gender.

AFFIRMATIVE ACTION:
focus on numbers

> If you don't like affirmative action, what is your plan to guarantee a level playing field of opportunity? —MAYNARD JACKSON,
> POLITICIAN

I often wondered if the Committee on Representation is our denomination's version of affirmative action.

According to Frank Wu, a law professor at Howard University, though affirmative action is not a perfect solution, the intention behind it is equality and integration. The hope is to begin to counter the disequilibrium that has occurred for hundreds of years in this society, mostly in those spheres of life that are affected by class and economic status, race and culture, and gender, among many issues. Wu writes, "Affirmative action is the applied component of the commitment to work toward achieving a society that not only happens to be racially diverse but also strives to be egalitarian and inclusive."[1]

I appreciate the opportunities given to me that were most likely the result of affirmative action efforts, ones that I believe I would not have experienced or acquired because my ability or talent might have been downplayed because, plain and simple, I am a minority. Perhaps there were no minorities in that position previous to my inquiry, or there were no women who served in that particular capacity. Whatever the reason, whether a lack of history or lack of imagination, without affirmative action, I would not have as much of a chance as others. It took me a long time to admit that reality. I always upheld the American ideal of equal opportunity for anyone and everyone. But, like any ideal, what occurred was often very different from the dream.

~~~~

While some may have not appreciated the value of this plan and reject anything that focuses on anything BUT merit, intelligence, and standards applied equally to everyone—the intentional system that ensures a broad spectrum of people are represented in whatever community—I have taken full advantage of it. To me, this is a way for me to assert my power, though it may be subversive and even hidden at times. When people question me and these so-called methods, I tell people, "Don't knock the hustle." I will play the game. I will respect the players. But I will not let the system own me. I will work the system to my benefit, and in the end, it will be beneficial to more people like me. I strongly believe that this is what it takes and will continue to be necessary in the future to change the overall institution of racism in this country.

—ANONYMOUS CLERGYWOMAN

~~~~

And so the affirmative action effort by my denomination has helped to initiate awareness. Often women of color experience what I call a double silence. It is not only one's skin color or ethnicity but gender that doubly binds us up and causes us to be invisible to the wider culture. But with affirmative action we are a much more visible demographic in many spheres of work and life. People are becoming more aware of the talents and abilities of those who are normally underrepresented whether in colleges or in church communities.

> Only [the one] who can see the invisible can do the impossible.
> —FRANK L. GAINES, FORMER MAYOR OF BERKELEY, CALIFORNIA

Awareness is essential, and is a helpful starting point. But what is also necessary beyond simply seeing is dialogue. The interfacing, interaction, and connection between people, particularly those who are in the center and those on the periphery, are transformative, not only for individuals but also for whole communities. Programs such as anti-racism training workshops are an important step toward conversations that are not easy or natural but that need to happen in order for real change to occur at institutional levels.

I had never felt comfortable talking about my race and ethnicity. As a Korean American I was always taught not to rock the boat. It was all about keeping my head down, nose to the grind, and working as hard as possible—this was the secret to success and having everything turn out fine. But it did not all turn out fine. I saw so many inequities all around me—from the lack of women in leadership in my home church, to never seeing a woman preach from the pulpit until I went away to college and visited my father, who was attending seminary at the time. I could not remove myself from those conversations about race and gender any longer if I were truly to be faithful to God.

A dear friend was part of a group who started the first anti-racism training at the seminary. I was inspired by the experience but also saddened by the scarcity of non-minorities present. I later heard many of the few attendees who were not minorities say somewhat condescending and disparaging things about the purpose and necessity for the training. I was shocked. Speechless. I could not believe that these people would be my colleagues in ministry someday. How could we possibly bring God's kingdom to bear in the world when we could hardly manage it in our own student community?

There is so much work to be done. It is not an easy issue, and there is definitely so much more that complicates it.

AUTHENTIC ALLIANCE:
focus on network

Cooperation is the thorough conviction that nobody can get there unless everybody gets there. —VIRGINIA BURDEN TOWER, THE PROCESS OF INTUITION

While I cannot downplay the importance of regulating diversity, I also cannot help but ask if we too easily dismiss what it means that we continue to need such a committee in the first place, especially in our supposed postfeminist and postracist society? As briefly mentioned above, the other side of affirmative action is the tendency toward tokenism. Perhaps part backlash and part natural consequence, I would often find myself the token, like a good placeholder in those endeavors for diversity, more like a trophy or medal that expressed whatever group was now truly progressive and therefore sensitive to the plight of silenced minority cultures and groups in society. But my ability or talent, my perspective, and my voice were downplayed in so many ways because they were not deemed necessary. My being Asian or a woman or young was good enough.

Though I appreciated the opportunity for a place at the table, it often felt forced and awkward. And I hardly ever spoke up. I did not think it was important for me to say anything, and mostly I felt my being there was a formality—no one could possibly care about my opinion or perspective. I approached meetings with a dread because they were vocational obligations, and so I always looked forward to the end, whether of the meeting or the term. But after the first few years of my journey as an ordained minister, my husband encouraged me to see them as learning opportunities, as well as a chance to offer something new and unexpected. He reminded me that the church *needs* my voice, and for me to exhibit God's faithfulness, it would mean stepping out of the boat even if I did not necessarily want to rock it.

I had a hard time living into this role. I often vacillated between both extremes. Sometimes, it felt presumed that I would need to assimilate into the local culture in order to be heard or understood by the committee of even my own congregation members. So, I tried to adopt the voice, mannerisms, and authority of the other members on the committee. Of course, that did not work well for me. I felt even more self-conscious and wondered if I would seem like a fraud. When I went the other direction and tried to speak up honestly, sometimes it felt that what I was saying was completely radical. I wondered if others thought I was a raging liberal. Even if another committee member would say something similar, it seemed to find better reception. I cannot help but think that this happened not because of the message but because of the messenger.

One of my favorite novels, *East of Eden* by John Steinbeck, speaks of this phenomenon. There's a telling scene between Samuel and Lee, the Chinese servant who is with the family, about Lee's (exaggerated) Chinese accent:

> *Lee looked at him and the brown eyes under their rounded upper lids seemed to open and deepen until they weren't foreign any more, but man's eyes, warm with understanding. Lee chuckled. "It's more than a convenience," he said. "It's even more than self-protection. Mostly we have to use it to be understood at all."*
>
> *Samuel showed no sign of having observed any change. "I can understand the first two," he said thoughtfully, "but the third escapes me."*
>
> *Lee said, "I know it's hard to believe, but it has happened so often to me and to my friends that we take it for granted. If I should go up to a lady or a gentleman, for instance, and speak as I am doing now, I wouldn't be understood."*
>
> *"Why not?"*
>
> *"Pidgin they expect, and pidgin they'll listen to. But English from me they don't listen to, and so they don't understand it."*
>
> *"Can that be possible? How do I understand you?"*
>
> *"That's why I'm talking to you. You are one of the rare people who can separate your observation from your preconception. You see what is, where most people see what they expect."*

The authentic connection between Samuel and Lee is one that exhibits God's kingdom to me. To truly see what is, rather than what is expected or falls under certain stereotypes and categories, and then to affirm, encourage, and make space. Affirmative action was never meant to be a permanent solution because it too easily turns into a diluted form of community where tokenism is the adhesive. But the existence of real network, where the focus is not on numbers or statistics and where people are truly tied up together in all the messes and complications, this is God's kingdom of radical existence rooted in love and grace.

This was something impressed upon me recently in ministry, and particularly in my life as a clergywoman of color. We need each other's voices. We do not need numbers. We do not need quotas. We do not even need goals or standards. We need each other. We need each other's experiences. We need each other's dreams. We need each other's stories. The kingdom of God is not a formula, it is not a committee, and it certainly is not meant to even look utopic and perfect. It is beautifully chaotic and interesting, and meant to be rich and full. And that means that I have to fully be myself wherever I am, no matter how hard or strange, no matter who can see or hear me.

> In dealing honestly with the problem of difference and the dream of pluralist feminism, I trust that we can be together where the Holy Spirit, our Divine Wisdom, our Sancta Sophia is both Hostess and Guest. With this hope I advocate the vision and the perspective which encompasses our coming to believe in the possibility of a variety of experiences, a variety of ways of understanding the world, a variety of frameworks of operation, without imposing consciously or unconsciously a notion of the norm. —TOINETTE M. EUGENE, IN *FEMINIST THEOLOGICAL ETHICS: A READER*

Notes
1. Frank Wu, *Yellow* (New York: Perseus Books Group, 2002), 8.

6
dancing the boundaries
THE STRUGGLE WITH FAMILY

ERICA LIU WITH MIHEE KIM-KORT

Hard times require furious dancing. Each of us is proof. —ALICE
WALKER, *HARD TIMES REQUIRE FURIOUS DANCING: NEW POEMS*

Worshiping with family is a challenge. I see the reasons why many
parents seem slightly distracted during the worship service, particularly when they have young children. I started praying with my
eyes open because the imperative to embrace the darkness and
quiet is just not feasible anymore. One of four things happens
when I close my eyes, particularly for prayer:

1. I start snoring.
2. I start daydreaming.
3. I start mentally composing lists.
4. The babies run away and/or fall off a pew (namely, in church
   on Sundays).

So I stopped closing my eyes. Actually, I stopped a while ago.
Mostly because of #2 and #3. But I also thought opening my eyes
would help me feel more connected to the people around me,
as well as to God. I found that sometimes in the midst of prayer
when my eyes were closed, it felt like the people praying with me

66

were far away—the sounds of voices seemed small and distant. Opening my eyes and looking around began to anchor me to the shared moment once I could let go of feeling sneaky or like I was breaking rules.

Now, though, when I'm juggling the babies during worship, it's an absolute necessity to keep my eyes. Wide. Open. While they toddle around the sanctuary. While they flap their hands and wave bulletin inserts loudly like pom poms in the air. While they laugh and shriek and call out for Daddy in his flowing black robe in the front. While they lean on the backs of the pews to poke the people in their faces. Yes, certainly it's distracting. Not just to me, either, and one might wonder how in the world I could possibly be present?

But I think that this season of faith—including the experience of prayer and worship—it is meant to be a different feeling. Worshiping as a parent requires a different energy and a more deliberate posture in worship. It is definitely much more exhausting in a way, and yet, at the same time, I find it is more tangible. To be present in that moment, in that community, as my children occupy the space, it feels like a form of faithfulness—the kind that is really associated with worship. And when I look around and see the community around me—and surrounding all the children—I cannot help but feel grateful. Joyful. Hopeful. Worshipful. And mindful of my desperately needful ways. Desperately needing to work toward the good of God's kingdom. I really believe this urgency comes from the connection experienced in prayer.

And I'm discovering it in new ways, and discovering the ways it's changing me.

Prayer is not asking for what you think you want, but asking to be changed in ways you can't imagine. —KATHLEEN NORRIS, POET AND AUTHOR

I have heard this said in so many ways. It is a reminder that I get to see the ways they are constantly changing before my eyes. And, ultimately I am being changed in ways that are beyond the horizons of my vision. Likewise, whether in my faith journey or vocational calling, my family is a huge part of how I embody this office and, more literally, how I occupy the worship space, the pulpit or pews, and the church. —MKK

My breasts were leaking. The final song of worship had barely finished as I made a beeline out of the sanctuary and then rushed upstairs to my office, where I swept my infant daughter from the babysitter's arms. After shooing her out the door with my older daughter, I closed the door so I could attend to serving communion a second time in private, this time giving literally of my own body to nourish my child.

As I sank into my seat to nurse, I wondered how I had come to this place. I was exhausted, not only sleep-deprived but also weary from running from one role to the next. I could feel myself disappearing under the weight of each of them—mother, spouse, pastor— and I began to consider if I had fallen into the same rut I had spent much of my young adult life trying to climb out of so desperately.

BECOMING ASIAN AMERICAN:
discovering my racial and christian identity

The value systems of those with access to power and of those far removed from such access cannot be the same. The viewpoint of the privileged is unlike that of the underprivileged. —AUNG SAN SUU KYI, WINNER OF THE NOBEL PEACE PRIZE

As an Asian American growing up in Silicon Valley, my sense of identity was late in blooming. Many emigrant families from East Asia had settled in the area with hopes of giving their children better access to the American dream. My friends and I were part of the second-generation that felt the weight of our parents' expectation. We spent much of our time together, but we also mixed easily with the Caucasian kids. As minorities we knew we were different, but rarely did we engage in explicit conversation about race in the United States.

This did not mean there was an absence of a color caste at school, however, even if it was not spoken aloud. It broke down in such a stereotypical way—the "smart kids" were Asian, the "popular kids" were white, the black kids (the few there were) were athletes, and so on. As high school girls desperately wanting to be thought of as pretty, my Asian American friends and I engaged in attempts to "whiten" ourselves as we strived to look like the models in *Seventeen* magazine. It was common among my friends to wear colored contacts (blue was a stretch, but very light brown and violet were popular), bleach their hair, and even get cosmetic surgery to gain the coveted, European double eyelid. Standards of beauty were decidedly white in everyone's minds, among both the Caucasian and Asian American students.

At some point in my adolescence, however, the stereotypes of Asian females expanded beyond nerdy smart girl to include hypersexual and exotic images. As insecure teenage girls who craved the validation of our beauty, we did not necessarily dodge that stereotype. We were too relieved at being asked to Homecoming to worry about how we were being oppressed. Along with the model minority image, we did not ever really question these typecast roles because we did not understand the deeper implications of the racist identifications.

During my time in college, a place where I might have experienced a racial awakening, I instead became an evangelical Christian. I joined a predominantly white group on campus, and it became a way to relieve some of the tension I felt existed between the Asian and American parts of my identity. Claiming a purely Christian identity was a way to bury that struggle and feel accepted into the dominant group. I started dating a white male from the community whom I eventually married, and together we decided to pursue a calling into ministry. It was while we were in seminary that I began to seriously question the premise of my identity and to realize that I had been "playing white" to gain approval.

It was an early experience in graduate school that opened my eyes to the roles I had been blindly acting. When we first arrived, I decided to check out two student groups; one was what you could characterize as the white, evangelical students, the other, the Asian American students. After attending a meeting of both groups, I realized that had I actually been blind, the only way I would have been able to tell the difference between the two was by the snacks they served afterwards. They used the same songs and preached the same theology, but the Asian group went out to a Korean restaurant instead of eating donuts and coffee. I started to grow uncomfortable with just these two options which narrowed me in different ways. The Asian group was dominated by the males, and it seemed that the women were not fully supported in becoming ordained pastors. The white group was, well, white, and clearly I was not.

Thus began a journey to discard the stereotypes, racist expectations, and given identities that were not of my own making. It was hard, more than a little scary, and though I felt freer I also felt somewhat unmoored. Who was I without all those roles to play? In community with other women of color, I started to find my voice. With trepidation at first, but later with more confidence, I rejected the geisha, submissive daughter, and model minority roles and began to sing out a new tune. I was energized and stirred by rereading the stories of foreign women who lived at the margins of society in the Bible—Rahab (Joshua 2), Ruth, and the unnamed Caananite woman (Matthew 15:21-28). Not because they provided a model of how to be a minority woman, but because of how God used them despite the marginalization they faced. It was an exhortation to embrace being an Asian American woman whom God could and wanted to use to do important work.

It was a season of transformation and pioneering—no longer trying to be white, but unsure of how to express myself because there were no models that I could see. It was coming to terms with the ways I had subsumed myself in order to survive in a dominant culture and finding strength to break free so I could bring my full self to the picture. With the support of other women of color, I found the space to try out new expressions of myself and to stand up against those who would dismiss or try to invalidate my voice because it was different. I also discovered God's affirmation, indeed I would even say pleasure, that I was starting to live into the person God had created me to be.

BECOMING MY VOCATION:
claiming my name as pastor

Of course I did not make this journey in a vacuum; my white husband was along for the ride. Along with negotiating my burgeoning identity as a proud woman of color, we were trying to figure out what it looked like to be pastors while navigating the added complexity of doing it together. Ask any young clergy what it is like to be newly ordained and they will have stories of the bumpy transition into that role. I was confronted with the additional challenge that I did not fit the traditional image of a pastor (namely, older white male), and I was doing it with my partner.

Our first call to ordained ministry was as co-pastors. We had always envisioned serving together, so it was an exciting opportunity. I had some reservations, however; though we were entering our new call as equals on paper, I was anxious about being mistaken as the pastor's wife or helpmate. While I technically *was* the pastor's wife, I did not want to be viewed as an appendage to my husband. When we first married, I had taken my spouse's surname, but it had always felt like an Anglo mask that somehow concealed an important part of my ethnic identity. As we began ministering together, I decided to reclaim my maiden name, Liu, as a visible sign of my own pastoral calling. It was a symbolic step, one that marked the transformation I had undergone from shame to pride, a purposeful discarding of whiteness and an embracing of my own heritage as honorable.

Our particular call was to campus ministry, working with students from a large, public university in the Midwest. In general, despite a small minority population on campus, I found the climate to be fairly open. Younger people had less trouble getting my gender and color in the role of pastor than older generations. Most of the time I encountered questions of my legitimacy, it came from folks in churches who made assumptions based on my appearance. Like the elderly woman who sidled up to me during a regional gathering and proceeded to tell me how she worked with foreign students for many years, complimented me on my English, and asked what country I was from; or the older, white, male pastor who refused to acknowledge my presence when talking to my husband and me at a clergy gathering; or the numerous church members who exclaimed how excited they were that I was on campus because I would be able to reach out to the international students given my background, which they assumed to be foreign despite the fact I was born in California. For the most part, students on campus were more reserved in voicing such assumptions and perhaps a little more open to seeing a young woman of color as their pastor.

But that does not mean it has not been a struggle. Given my background and experiences, I longed to serve in a more multicultural context and often wondered what in the world I was doing, working with all these white students who thought they had come to the big, diverse city. I worried that they would regard my white spouse as more legitimate than myself (a not completely unfounded suspicion) and was troubled by the notion that I might be selling out by serving in this context. After being surrounded by women of color during my trek through seminary, I found myself isolated. Doubt gnawed at me as I tried to live fully into my identity as a female pastor of color without a community to support and walk with me.

I found encouragement in phone calls and Skype sessions with my sisters in ministry across the nation and connected with a community in Chicago that I visited periodically. I was reminded that God's call never guarantees the people you serve will look like you, and in fact God might use that difference to build bridges and foster reconciliation. Over time, I became less self-conscious about being the only non-white person in the room and more comfortable talking about my ethnic heritage and experience of being a minority in America as a critical part of my spiritual formation. There came a time, not one that I can pinpoint, that seeing my name, Reverend Erica Liu, became natural and normal—not just to myself but to those all around me.

BECOMING MY SECOND VOCATION: motherhood

In a child's eyes, a mother is a goddess. She can be glorious or terrible, benevolent or filled with wrath, but she commands love either way. I am convinced that this is the greatest power in the universe. —N. K. JEMISIN, *THE HUNDRED THOUSAND KINGDOMS*

Just before we accepted the call to serve as co-pastors, I gave birth to our first child. The ministry was in Wisconsin, not a place I ever imagined living and one I felt apprehensive about because I did not want to raise our children in an environment where they would be anomalies. Having recently come into my own racial-ethnic awareness, I did not want them to grow up in a place where being white was normative. I worried they would view their own ethnic heritage as somehow less than or even something to hide. Moving to the middle of the country felt in some ways like a betrayal to all I had worked hard to overcome. It was with more than a little apprehension that we settled our new family in the Midwest.

Once we arrived, however, these anxieties promptly were put on the back burner as I simply tried to survive. The first few years of raising my children felt like a continual Ironman, the triathlon which consists of a 2.4-mile swim, 112-mile bike ride, and 26.2-mile run. Becoming a mother was the most demanding rite of passage I have ever endured. While I loved my children, the maternal way of moving about did not come easily to me (only the anxiety came naturally). It was a shock to the system and was complicated by the fact that I was also simultaneously becoming a pastor.

Of all the roles I have taken on, motherhood has been the most challenging and complex. There is no shortage of opinions on how to be a good mother; the extra layers of being a mother of color have also meant sifting through unhelpful stereotypes. Images like Miss Saigon's portrayal of a mother who would go so far as to kill herself to give her child a chance to live in America; Tiger mom who would go to any lengths to make sure her daughters would be the best of the best; or countless women of color who would sacrifice their unique personhood for the sake of their children, and even for other people's children. Parenting is a vocation inherent with sacrifice, but there is an added burden for mothers of color. While it is still difficult for white moms to be CEOs, when they do attain such a position it is usually a given that back at home there is a nanny of color taking care of the children. There is an assumption that women of color naturally fit into this role.

The transition to becoming a mother and a pastor was a bumpy road, especially given these dynamics. The roles of pastor and mother share a lot in common—nurturing, teaching, guiding, soothing wounds, comforting, loving—but most people do not look at these skills in a woman and conclude that mothers would make natural pastors. In fact, these traits in a female clergy of color are perceived differently than if they were recognized in a traditional, white male pastor. Where one might be identified as pastoral, the other might be classified as maternal and emotional. Indeed, when I was going through my final assessment for ordination, one of the older men on the committee commented on how I had a very maternal presence during my sermon. All the committee members were aware that I had a young infant at home, and it seemed to be the dominant image for some. Not sure what to make of this feedback, I was relieved when a female committee member interjected that what she observed was a strength and assertiveness. I let the two of them debate it out but left wondering how these two roles would play off of each other in my life.

On the one hand, the role of pastor generally means an upfront presence, a highly visible leadership position, and for better or worse, the greatest influence in the life of the church. On the other hand, mothers are often relegated to the background, especially mothers of color, and for the most part do not seem to have much voice at all. The combination of these two vocations in one person is not expected, and frequently people would latch onto my identity as a mother rather than see me as a pastor. Perhaps that made it easier for them to dismiss me.

Making it more complicated, I was also trying to figure out how to navigate these roles with my spouse and partner in ministry. The ongoing "mommy wars" in society, admittedly only among the privileged women who have a choice about working or staying home with the children, was a conversation I did not engage in until I came out of the fog of infancy. My own mother had always worked full-time when I was growing up, while my spouse grew up with a stay-at-home mom. My first pregnancy was a happy surprise for both of us, so while we both assumed one of us should be home with the kids, we had not discussed who would take on this role. When, at the beginning of our first call, we still had not managed to get our baby on a bottle, it seemed the path of least resistance for me to go part-time in my work so that I could be the one at home and continue nursing.

By the time our second child came along a few years later, I was still working part-time and watching my spouse's career develop and grow. While I was proud of him, I started to feel unsettled by my own seeming stagnation and fading into the background. We had tough conversations about the parent-work balance and the negotiation of each other's vocational aspirations. I do not believe that anyone can have it all without someone else picking up the tab to make it possible; any parent knows that raising children is an all-out and all-consuming endeavor that does not mesh well with an all-out and all-consuming career. I needed my sacrifices to be acknowledged not as a given—as if I were expected to subsume myself for the family's sake—but as an intentional choice made from a place of power, my own power. My spouse agreed that I had given up some of my own vocational growth in order for our children to be primarily taken care of by one of us; I accepted that this was going to be a season in my life but not an eternal one. At some point, we would shift the scales of balance for it to be my turn; in the meantime, we would find ways to honor this particular period when I chose to be the one who was at home for the kids more of the time than at work. This allowed me to embrace my second vocation in mothering with a sense of empowerment rather than feeling that a role was being imposed upon me.

BECOMING WHOLE:
mother God

Mother is the name for God in the lips and hearts of little children. —WILLIAM MAKEPEACE THACKERAY, *VANITY FAIR*

At first, the combination of the pastoral and mothering vocations threatened to bury me and I started to feel as if I simply existed to fulfill other people's expectations. It was not so much that I had put on the white mask again, but I became too overwhelmed to do anything other than survive. It was during one of the many episodes of hiding in my office to nurse my young child, however, that I began to discern an image that breathed new life into my soul and gave me another way to envision who I was becoming.

Any mother who has breastfed a young infant has experienced the relentless demand to feed an often wailing, hungry, and desperate little mouth. There is an accompanying ache that matches those cries, with an actual physical pain that comes from the fullness of milk waiting to be released. Once a baby has latched on to a mother's breast to eat, it takes a few moments before the milk starts to flow. Eventually the baby calms with the filling of her tummy and soothing that comes with being held securely in her mother's arms. And then a peace settles after mother has given of her very own body to give life to her child.

In our worshipping community, we celebrate the Lord's Supper every week, so the words of institution are mantras that regularly roll off my tongue. While trying to manage the two separate dances of leading worship and nursing my child, I unexpectedly found the two had related rhythms that blended together to make a new dance for me to step into. *This is my body, given for you; this is my blood shed for you. Take and eat, take and drink.*

These words had a new resonance after becoming a mother who knew intimately what it meant to give of her own body to nurture a young soul. I saw Jesus in a new way, not only as host of this meal but also as Mother God who demonstrated leadership and power in a radically different way than tradition dictated. These were images that integrated the vocations I had been struggling to balance, mother and minister, and allowed me to embody the roles on terms more authentic to my being.

This has given me the opportunity to reset what is normative when it comes to these vocational roles. For my children, it is ordinary for a pastor to be a petite, Asian American woman who is also a mother—in fact, that is their primary image of mother and pastor. They expect a space in the pastor's office where their stash of toys permanently resides, and they are used to seeing their mother lead many other people, including folks who do not look like them. For the members in the worshipping community where I minister, they are receiving a fuller picture of Mother-Father God as I share insights from a perspective not usually voiced. Bringing these vocations together breaks down the artificial walls that can creep up between people, especially because folks are not used to the combination of young, Asian American, female, mother, co-pastor in one person. I don't fit into traditional boxes, and it forces others to reevaluate the usefulness of these boxes in the first place.

Of course, figuring out the rhythm of this complex dance still means there are times I find myself out of sync or taking a few missteps. As there are different tempos and movements that make up a piece, I have also realized there are various periods in my life I need to distinguish and respect for it to be a sustainable, life-long dance.

Accepting this grace has been critical in negotiating the multifaceted vocational roles in my life.

In every person's life, there are many different seasons. There is a certain wisdom that comes with recognizing that having it all at the same time produces craziness rather than a feeling of wholeness; most folks would agree a blizzard in July signals that something is amiss. Having this perspective helped me to relax a little while I read *Goodnight Moon* for the hundredth time while colleagues were attending conferences, writing books, or taking on positions of significant leadership. I have been learning to appreciate the particular seasons I find myself in, knowing that there will be different ones ahead.

Most of all, it has created space for me to move about this dance in the way I am uniquely made to move. As a person who claims a hyphenated identity, I have spent my life straddling the boundary lines rather than staying neatly to one side or the other. This means I have the freedom to make up my own steps that lie outside of anybody else's definitions of these particular roles I inhabit. And that has been liberating because the reality is that none of us resides in singular roles but rather dances among several. I am no longer confined by a lock-step expectation to fulfill these various roles on other people's terms; instead, I choose to dance to my own unique rhythms.

7

the other pastor

THE STRUGGLE WITH LEGITIMACY

LARISSA KWONG ABAZIA

As a child of immigrant parents, as a woman of color in a white society, and as a woman in a patriarchal society, what is personal to me is political. —Mitsuye Yamada

Here is what I imagine it must have been like in the early years of the disciples' ministry: A group of young believers walk down the street and stumble upon a leper begging for change. One eager disciple reaches out an arm only to be met with a strong grasp on the wrist.

"I'm sorry. Is Peter available? It's just that, well, I've heard so much about him . . ."

The disciple pauses to allow the familiar wave of emotions—insecurity, uncertainty, indignation, rejection—wash over her as she responds with a shake of the head.

"All right," the leper says with a disappointed sigh. "You'll do, then."

SECOND CLASS: being the junior pastor

When the associate-senior relationship works, it is a beautiful way to do ministry. And when that relationship is broken, it can be as painful a rupture as the unraveling of a family relationship. The intimacy and intensity of this work make the stakes so high. —LILLIAN DANIEL, IN *THIS ODD AND WONDROUS CALLING*

Challenging power dynamics exist between heads of staff and associate pastors. Some are created among colleagues; others arise in the form of triangulation between staff and congregation members with personal motives; and the associate pastors live into the dynamics connected with the job titles themselves.

I was realistic about the challenges and potential pitfalls of this relationship as I served a congregation in Chicago, Illinois, as its first associate pastor. Many of the accounts that I heard from colleagues serving as associates elsewhere rang true during my time with the congregation. But my situation was further complicated as a woman of color, not only struggling with the existing power dynamics in the role as other pastor but also with culture differences as an other clergywoman in a predominately white context.

I first learned of the concept of liminality (a threshold or in-between existence) in my second year of seminary, and it helped to define the uncomfortable feelings of being an outsider throughout my life. No doubt many Asian Americans have at least one story of being asked, "Where are you from?" followed almost immediately by, "No, I mean where are you *really* from?" We are familiar with feedback that our English is "so clear" and that we are surprisingly articulate, leaving absent the fact that many of us were born and raised in the United States with English as a primary language. As those living in a liminal state, we will always look like foreigners in our own land yet will never fully fit in our cultural homelands, either. Neither American nor Asian, we are forced to inhabit an in-between space, liminal homes that are never fully in one or the other. While looking like a perpetual foreigner in my birthplace, the same could be said for my place in the church. Nowhere is this as clear as in my theological beliefs and their effects on my ministry.

One of our greatest struggles as human beings is our inherent ability to see difference. Despite this natural tendency, as the faithful, we are challenged to live in community that embraces all people despite race, class, education, sexuality, age, gender, and any other differences that we see or experience. This isn't a surprising theological understanding in Christian circles; however, the results of this inclusivity on a practical level define the congregational context in which I found myself in Chicago. I served a More Light congregation there, which in Presbyterian circles signifies a community open to and affirming of LBGTQ men and women. The congregation was dedicated to social justice work and reached out not only to its neighborhood but also throughout the world. This desire to be open, welcoming, and justice-oriented was a perfect match to my ministerial call, but it involved serving a predominantly white congregation.

My background and experience growing up in a congregation where my family *was* the diversity in its numbers led me to believe that I could serve a congregation regardless of its racial or ethnic makeup. I was keenly aware that associate pastors struggle to exert authority and are often seen as the other pastor—someone who is to learn from the head of staff but is not expected to contribute to the life of the congregation in the same ways as the senior pastor. Yet I was not prepared to have to face my otherness as a Chinese American young adult in the church. I could look out in the congregation at any given worship, meeting, or Bible study and experience some diversity, but for the most part, I began to observe how I was different from those I was trying to serve. My cultural background was dissimilar, and yet it was what provided a foundational approach to my theology and teaching. As a result, I embarked on a journey of otherness rooted in not only my pastoral role but also my personal identity.

Take the first day with any congregation, and the initial thing people notice about their new pastor is how he or she compares with those who came before. In my case, as an associate, I was contrasted with the head of staff; as a thirty-something woman of color with experience in the national level of my denomination and a passion for racial justice work, I was quite different. I was different not only outwardly but also inwardly. My call to ministry, experiences in seminary, and understandings of congregational community were all different and formed by my experiences as a Chinese American woman. As a person of color, I was familiar with the feeling of choosing which identity or identities to bear without expressing my whole self if the environment lacked safe space. It is not surprising that I saw my difference as an initial liability to my work. I could speak, act, and lead as the congregation expected, but there was always an inner voice asking if it was really me or a shadow doing what was necessary to serve in the pastoral role. Could I be myself *and* serve as an associate pastor in a majority white congregation?

SECOND SPACE:
creating a venue for ministry

> Throw your dreams into space like a kite, and you do not know what it will bring back, a new life, a new friend, a new love, a new country. —ANAÏS NIN, AUTHOR AND ACTOR

One of my favorite Scripture passages is the interaction between the Syrophonecian woman and Jesus in Mark's Gospel. A Greek woman outside of Jesus' culture and context, she finds him attempting to rest from his travels and ministry efforts. She is determined to have the young rabbi heal her demon-possessed daughter, yet Jesus initially denies her request. Without hesitation the woman responds, "Lord, even the dogs underneath the table eat the children's crumbs" (Mark 7:28, CEB).

Jesus had surrounded himself with those of his culture, hoping to reclaim the ancient Jewish faith that had long strayed from its foundational principles. This Gentile mother respected his desire to support his own people but reminded him that even the crumbs from the Jewish table would be welcome to the Gentiles who were deemed outsiders. Her determination paid off, and Jesus changed his mind, healing the young girl even before her mother arrived home.

Space to grow, change, stumble, and explore is necessary in any role and particularly for new clergy, be they associate or not, and whether they are other in race, age, gender, sexuality, or any other way. Sometimes that space may not seem readily available, especially within the confines of a church's long-held traditions and rituals. Likewise, that space may already be occupied by others—other pastors, other leaders, even memories and histories of past clergy. It is all too easy to feel like an outsider, and while this might be a natural part of the process for integrating into a community, sometimes this feeling remains much longer than necessary. Sometimes these differences become definitions of one's place in the community.

While associate pastors are not always outsiders in race, culture, and gender like the Syrophonecian woman and I, our roles can sometimes pit us against our head of staff in an authoritarian hierarchy. Such a structure may allow a parishioner or lay leader to ask a question of an associate pastor but then require that person (formally or tacitly) to verify the answer with the senior pastor. If a particularly important pastoral care need arises, many leaders will assume that the head of staff should attend to it, believing that he or she is the face that the affected family desires—far more so than the other pastor. A senior pastor's vacation or study leave gives the associate a bit more breathing room to do things his or her own way. And as time goes by and the associate feels more freedom to experiment creatively in worship or teaching, often congregation members assume that the new idea or program is the handiwork of the head of staff—or at least that he or she had an important hand in implementing it despite the role of the associate pastor.

On the other hand, when a new staff member is allowed space to express fully himself or herself, it offers an immediate opportunity for a fresh set of eyes on the congregation. Inevitably, the associate pastor will see and experience the church differently, but the difference in this case does not have to be negative. In fact, this is a gift to the congregation. It requires courage and conviction for the associate to stand behind what he or she sees and experiences, but such a stand will allow the community to grow because of the associate's unique perspective, a perspective made unique because of the associate's individual identity as a human being, with contrasting experiences of life and culture, and because of the associate's functional position on the leadership team, with different experiences of the congregation. In many situations the rare glimpse into congregational life that the associate pastor offers becomes a missed opportunity. The potential for the congregation to become stagnant increases if this gift remains unopened.

I have spent most of my life navigating the waters of both Chinese and North American culture that flow inside of me. One of the more challenging dynamics is the balance between the rugged individualism of the United States and the implicit honor of parents and elders maintained in Asian cultures. Americans naturally gravitate toward individualism that perpetuates everything within its society.

While the Christian church upholds a countercultural emphasis on community and the necessity of the body of Christ, these US cultural ideals can often seep into church culture. For instance, it is too easy to praise individuals for their work rather than the team or committee—the head of coffee hour rather than the volunteers, or the pastor who conceived the new plan rather than the people who implemented and expanded the initiative. Likewise, US culture affirms that hard work and determination are all that one needs to be successful. The emphasis continues to be on highlighting only ability and intelligence, and ultimately qualifications. Asian Americans believe this as well, but the decisions that individuals make are consistently weighed through the needs of the whole. The input of one's elders, the needs of the family, and the ramifications of the potential decision beyond oneself are all weighed before an answer. These divergent ideals became particularly problematic for me as an associate pastor.

Life as an associate pastor includes odd mathematics. I added up the benefits and challenges of saying or doing things and the repercussions they could have, both personally and professionally. I was torn daily by the desire to assert myself, coupled with an inherent belief that my head of staff was an elder who needed to be respected and followed; I was there to offer support and lead only in the roles dictated within my job description. Yet, even within my spheres of influence, I felt responsible continually to seek approval for decisions and ideas.

As I weighed things in my own mathematical formula, I let go of the unique voice that I offered to the congregation. I made myself wear different hats for the appropriate situation, missing the opportunity to embrace all the intersections of my identity with my ministry—and the gifts such intersections could offer. Yet, in the moments when I stood my ground, believing that I had a voice and experience that mattered, I made a difference in my ministry.

The church's neighborhood in Chicago is home to a substantial LGBTQ community, resulting in the rise of a community center for all ages as well as social services specifically geared toward youth. This openness in the neighborhood resulted in an unexpected influx of LGBTQ youth of color who fled from less welcoming areas or families who had disowned them. This resulted in an interesting dynamic for the community: the gentrified area with many young predominantly white families has had to wrestle with its openness to the increasing numbers youth of color occupying the sidewalks and public spaces. Police would target those youth, resulting in arrests with little or no reason beyond seeming out of place in the neighborhood. Divisions began to arise within the neighborhood as advocates for the youth were pitted against those who felt threated by their presence.

Several months before I arrived, the congregation decided to respond to the needs of the youth by opening the doors of their fellowship hall from 8 p.m. to midnight every Friday night. The new program became a safe social space for LGBTQ youth and their allies from ages sixteen to twenty-four. It is 100 percent volunteer-run and thrives only on the dedication of individuals giving their Friday nights to staff the space.

As time went on, several incidences of violence within the church's space on Friday nights caused a rift among the volunteers in the program. With more than ninety youth and several adult volunteers present each week, we were all learning how to share space and build relationships with one another. The at-risk youth walking through our doors would sometimes push our limits just to see how open we were to them; was it all talk, or were we living up to the openness that we proclaimed? In addition, divisions among the different groups of youth caused strife in the space. Only a few weeks before I started as the congregation's associate pastor, someone was injured during an incident, leading the volunteers and head of staff to decide to shut down the program for a month to regroup. One of my primary responsibilities when I came on staff was to oversee the continuation of the program.

While the congregation could be proud of its evening program, I recognized that we were also learning as we went along. I worked hard to lay a stronger foundation that would provide a safe space not only for the youth but also for all of the adults in the fellowship hall each evening. While many of the participants were youth of color, most of our volunteers were white. I intentionally asked each person during training, "Why do you want to volunteer for this program?"

More often than not, they would share their own experiences and desire to illustrate that the youth could be just as successful as they had. I never disagreed with any personal testimonies but emphasized that access to resources and experience of the contexts around them is quite different from the access available to the teens.

I had countless conversations with youth who didn't see a future for themselves beyond surviving the next year or two. Many of the participants in the program were homeless, with a survivor's focus on securing food and a safe place to sleep each night; they didn't have the luxury of working toward a specific successful career. They also had to deal with the intersection of their sexual and racial identities that made them even more of a minority in the neighborhood.

During volunteer trainings and other community interactions, I opened up the conversation whenever I could, emphasizing that we had to be careful about how we described and lived into the space, trying our best to not paint ourselves as saviors but as partners with the youth. Success, I would say, can be measured in different ways. We needed to acknowledge who the youth were as individuals and how their context shaped their realities. We could provide a positive influence in our lives, but we had to be partners in their futures *as they saw it* instead of projecting what we thought would be best for them.

This program became one of the ways that my experience as a young woman of color allowed me to become an authority in the shaping of a program. My life experience was significantly different from that of the teen participants, but I could relate to and express an understanding of their marginality when I talked about the program with the youth and with the church volunteers. It was within this context that I found my voice the strongest.

SECOND CHANCE:
following my own path

Destiny is not a matter of chance; it is a matter of choice.
—WILLIAM JENNINGS BRYANT, POLITICIAN AND FORMER
US SECRETARY OF STATE

I decided to leave my call as an associate pastor after almost four years of ministry. My mathematics had come down to this: the needs of the church had become greater than what I wanted to give of myself and at the neglect of my family. My son had become a casualty of evening meetings and increasing time in the office. At least once or twice a week, my husband would drive him from day care to the church alley so that I could kiss him on the forehead because he would be asleep well before I got home. I consistently checked emails and did work from home to maintain my ministries and offer pastoral care. The lines of personal and professional life were at odds, and work was becoming the clear winner, taxing my physical, emotional, and spiritual health.

I thought back to my parents as I added up the decision to leave the associate pastorate. My father came to the United States from mainland China when he was eleven. He served in the military, went to college, and worked hard so that my sister and I could have more opportunities than he was ever afforded. My mother grew up in New York City's Chinatown as the youngest and only daughter in her family, working hard to show that she could do just as much as her brothers. She fought against the gender stereotypes of her parents and proved that she was capable of both a professional and family life. They had worked so hard to give us access to our dreams. I believed that I had failed them.

I talked to my mother once about my choice to leave the associate pastor position. She was proud that I had not given into the job description which allowed me little input nto my responsibilities. She was encouraged that I had taken the step to stand up for myself and my family, instead of continuing to bow to the pressure as I had for much of my time with the congregation. I had not failed my family but made them proud for holding my ground and honoring my individual strengths that I had worked so hard to uncover.

As I filled out the form to seek a new call in the Presbyterian Church (USA), I reflected on the last narrative question: What are the key theological issues facing the church and society and how do they shape your ministry? I did not hesitate in my response, expounding on the challenges that difference creates in our congregations and society. Such reflection helped me realize that the difference I saw in myself was holding me back from fulfilling the exact role I feel called to fulfill. I constantly compared myself with my head of staff, worried that people would never move beyond seeing me as a sidekick to her ministry, and focused on the dynamics of our relationship instead of the unique gifts I brought to the community. The comparisons became the difference between effective ministry and insecurity.

I had spent a lot of time wondering about and working toward assimilating to the congregational context in which I found myself as an associate, instead of embracing the differences that my otherness brought to the congregation. I strategized as to what I could alter of myself and leave outside of the church doors to function successfully in my ministry. It wasn't until I left the church that I realized how much I had left behind each day simply to function.

I took a lot of my negative experiences as an associate pastor personally, viewing them as direct questions of my value to the congregation. They exist as significant symbols of the ways that my ministry was taken from me and how my voice was silenced. I felt left behind, having to chase after those who held power to prove that I deserved the ordination I worked so hard to earn.

After my departure, I realized that I possessed the power to push things out of the way and confidently take the seat I believed belonged to me. No one could give me the authority; I had to take it and own it on my own. That meant stepping into the assumed authority that infiltrates white privilege and embracing my own voice within it. Although contradictory to Asian culture's honor toward elders and its valued tradition of consistently seeing oneself as a partner for the good of the greater whole, my experience of white privilege taught me that I had to be more outspoken in order to demonstrate my knowledge and competence and to assert my authority. I had to speak up, or no one else would. I learned that my own feelings of silence were not isolated. Others in the congregation felt it too, and as a pastor, it was my responsibility to speak up in order to provide the safe space for their perspectives as well.

I truly believe it is our differences and otherness that shape us into the unique image of God that God intended to make us. We could not compose the whole body of the church without our different functions:

> For just as the body is one and has many members, and all the members of the body, though many, are one body, so it is with Christ. For in the one Spirit we were all baptized into one body—Jews or Greeks, slaves or free—and we were all made to drink of one Spirit. Indeed, the body does not consist of one member but of many. (1 CORINTHIANS 12:12-14, NRSV)

I have spent far too long asking myself why I do not fit into the body instead of living into the reasons that I do fit in my own way. As a Chinese American, I can speak to the significance of community that embraces individuality for the good of the whole. As a wife and mother, I can live into the challenging balance of home and work life. As a friend, I can grow through the laughter and guidance of those around me. As a clergywoman, I can teach and lead others through my experiences as a faithful believer. And in all of my identities interwoven together, I can bring everything that I am as a gift to the community to which I am called in whatever season.

I have spent far too long seeing my otherness as a liability as opposed to my greatest, God-given asset to those I serve. I have allowed myself to be silenced instead of speaking up as an associate pastor with a unique vision and voice. This was a loss, not only to my growth but also to the congregation I served, which never fully received the seeds that I could plant with them and the fruits that we could nurture together.

As I write this, I am preparing to embark on a new ministerial journey as pastor of a multiethnic, multicultural congregation in the heart of Queens, New York. While I have no idea what is in store for me there, I am excited about the ways that God will use all of us to the betterment of our congregational life together. We represent countless countries around the world and strive to work together to represent God's beloved community in the Forest Hills neighborhood. We all bring our otherness as a community of immigrants, first- and second-generation individuals, and those who have been in America for generations, and it is my priority to uphold our unique gifts and talents to reflect the body of Christ in the world.

This is only the continuation of my journey, leading me to something new that God has planned for the future. I would not be the leader I am today without my experiences as an associate pastor, both positive and negative. I am now able to take each story and see how I have grown from my first day to the last. And, more importantly, if I am ever in a situation where I work with an associate pastor, I will know how to learn from that other pastor as a partner in ministry.

8

what's my passion?

THE STRUGGLE WITH
DISCOVERING ONE'S NICHE

YANA J. PAGAN, LeQUITA HOPGOOD PORTER, FELICIA DEAS,
AND LAURA MARIKO CHEIFETZ WITH MIHEE KIM-KORT

I believe there's a calling for all of us. I know that every human being has value and purpose. The real work of our lives is to become aware. And awakened. To answer the call. —OPRAH WINFREY, MEDIA GIANT AND ACTOR

Don't underestimate your worth by comparing yourself with others. —JAACHYNMA N. E. AGU, *THE PRINCE AND THE PAUPER*

For my seminary application, it was a no-brainer when I had to fill in the section on my plans after graduation. There was not a shred of doubt in my mind about my desire to go into youth ministry, specifically at a Korean American church. I grew up loving the experience of my church family, including all its quirks and idiosyncrasies and even for its obvious imperfections, and I realized just how much the youth ministry influenced my life. It was not only the community of youth but also the way we were connected to the larger community. It felt real. It felt important and meaningful. And so, nothing else seemed to make sense as I filled in the sections on what I anticipated doing after seminary.

When I finally stepped foot on campus, even the air seemed to affirm every step I had taken to get there from my admission into the program back in December to my long road trip from Colorado to New Jersey. Everything made sense. Everything fell into place. Everything was exciting and full of so much potential. And then, classes started for the fall.

I was in the midst of juggling academically rigorous courses while redefining many of my beliefs and faith statements, and like many Asian American students, working for a church on the weekends. It was not an internship, like the second- and third-year students did for the year and for credit. (Typically, the local Korean churches find out who the new students are on campus, and as soon as they get a chance, they snatch them up like fish in a net and hire them as student pastors to work with their youth and children. Three churches approached me in the first week I was there for a summer language course. Another one contacted me in the fall after I had become available again, having served as an interim over the summer.) All this on top of the social life at the seminary, as well as meeting and dating the boy who would be my future husband, proved to overflow my cup in wonderful and demanding ways.

Some days it felt like I was drowning.

When the dust started to settle during my second year of seminary, I began to see other possibilities for ministry. I started to compare my interests with others. While I loved and enjoyed the age group of the elementary school students I was working with at a large Korean Presbyterian church, I could not help but wonder: What else?

What else was out there?

What else could I do?

What else might God call me to pursue with the gifts given to me?

I started to feel cramped. I have always abhorred being pigeon-holed when it came to my abilities or interests. But it felt like some unknown forces were slowly and subtly nudging me a certain way. And it did not always feel like the Holy Spirit. I started to appreciate the merit of having a specialty or field of concentration, for those situations that require particular expertise, and even for those jobs that have a clear focus and job description. Nonetheless, I still resisted being shoved into a single little cubby. Granted, I generally know—at least, I presume to know—what I enjoy in terms of work, and I know where my skills lie in terms of ministry, but I like to think that I am so much more. I like to think that I am capable of so much more. I like to think that there are so many more contingencies and occasions for creative ministry in the wider church.

However, the rare pragmatic side of me realizes that I will not be able to do it all and there is a reason for the professionalization of this vocation. So, I wonder: Is there a healthy balance between being well-rounded and focused? Being a generalist, or more specialized in one's job description and work? Being both definitive and creative or generative? Yana, LeQuita, Felicia, and Laura offer glimpses into this conversation through their own processes, and some windows into how we might also approach these questions in our own ministries. —MKK

NURTURING CALLING:
singing my story

YANA J. PAGAN

I think it all started when I was a little girl, in need of so much. People talked and did things I could not understand. Like many young girls I admired Wonder Woman, putting hair rollers around my wrist, tying a belt around my waist, and making my lasso of truth to get things done. I wanted to use my Wonder Woman strength to care for my brother who was ill with asthma, and with her strength I would stop being afraid that he would die, especially when his condition made him stop eating for weeks at a time.

Around that same time in my life, my grandfather gave me a guitar, and I used it to make melodies and create songs I would sing to God. My songs were songs of prayers asking God whom I did not know yet knew he was there to heal my brother. It was these prayers and songs to this God that challenged me or motivated me to keep on going. I also watched my grandmother do the same— take the guitar in her rocking chair and read the Bible, sing songs and hymns. We never went to church, yet every morning, afternoon, and evening she would say that we have to pray. She would cry in that chair, and she would talk and write and read Christian songs, and it is from her that I learned how to sing my praises, concerns, fears, to the one who cared for me.

Frances Crosby said it best with the song "Blessed Assurance" in 1873. This is my prayer: "This is my story, this is my song / Praising my Savior all the day long; / This is my story, this is my song, / Praising my Savior all the day long." Singing is how I wrestle with my God and discover my niche. I love the old hymns that tell a story, and "Blessed Assurance" is just one of many. I feel like this song writes about my journey with the One who calls me and assures me of God's promises.

How did I discover my passion, my niche? It has been a process in which I have learned by trial and error. Finding a voice in ministry has been one of difficulty, yet at the same time it's been one that I had to find in order to survive. I was raised by women, very strong women, I might add, who may not have been church leaders, but they were still heads of household and family. When I became a Christian later in my teens, I found that most people in the church were women. While that was not surprising, I was further encouraged that women were the primary leaders. In hindsight, I realize this female-centric experience was my cultural norm, even if I was not aware that my role in home and church was different, let's say, from that of my brother.

> Blessed assurance, Jesus is mine! Oh, what a foretaste of glory divine! Heir of salvation, Purchase of God, Born of His Spirit, washed in His blood. —FANNY CROSBY, "BLESSED ASSURANCE"

My church introduced me to my Savior, and my church also played a crucial role in my growth as a believer, really influencing me in such a way that it gave me confidence. When I left New York City to go to college, I was sure that God was calling me (yes, me) to be a pastor. What was most shocking to me in college was that it wasn't men only who were telling me that I should not be a woman in ministry; it was also my female counterparts.

I found that women were adamant and sometimes even painfully aggressive toward me in their words and actions about the fact that I was misled in my beliefs. It was as if their genre of music was the only one, and they expected me to sing the tune they sang. It still saddens me that people forget we are all created in God's image. Too many people limit God to gender, so one of my most-quoted verses is Galatians 3:28 (NKJV), "There is neither Jew nor Greek, there is neither slave nor free, there is no male and female, for you are all one in Christ Jesus."

While young and naïve, I did not know how to defend myself, but I was not convinced that they were correct or that I was wrong. Still, because this was the first time that I was being challenged that a woman should not be a pastor, I internalized their comments and negativity and became silently doubtful. I do not think many people realized that it was that first year of college that turned my confidence into questions. I clung to my own melody anyway, humming as best as I could, "Echoes of mercy, whispers of love." What I had gained in my early female-centric years now wrestled with self-doubt, and all that I had learned I now questioned its validity. I started to say things like, "Well, maybe I'm not called to be a pastor. Maybe I made a mistake."

I used to joke about being Yana, "Woman of Many Trades." Yet in recent years I realized that this is part of who I am. Because of my past and my present, there are many things that I am willing to take on as a challenge. The secret for me is to share my story. My past portrays the opposite of who I have become: a woman who has encountered a purpose in Christ and knows that God has a plan for me. I am a daughter of God, even though I am orphaned in many ways. I am an ordained ABCUSA clergywoman, a chaplain, a preacher, and a professor. I am a caretaker, but more than anything, I am called just as I am, a woman.

That was the story of the disciples. Jesus called them from where they were in their lives. Yet as a woman, at least for myself, I have always had this self-doubt that I am to be something else. I know that I am not alone in this sentiment, for too many women try to be someone other than the one they are meant to be as God's creation.

I have encountered many women who are okay with the fact that their only role is to teach women and children. I have never been able to swallow that way of thinking. I doubted my call, but I got involved in student chaplaincy in college, where I realized that God was using my leadership ability. From that point on, I continued to build relationships with people who were not just like

myself, and I became curious about how they came to their conclusions that women do not belong in ministry.

It was those relationships that helped me to continue to read
and study and find out more. It was because of my willingness to be
in relationship with others that I found it easy to discuss issues that
were different from my own. I learned a lot about myself in those
college relationships, which helped me realize there was more than
one opinion about many things in life. I came to the realization that
being willing to talk with others and listen to their stories and inviting them to hear my story could go so much further than bickering.

Another area in which I doubted myself was related to my
health. In my studies, I read about Charles Spurgeon, who said
that if one was ill one should not be a pastor. So, I wrestled again
with the idea of ministry, not because of my gender this time but
because I was sick. My chronic illness was yet another obstacle to
being called. Then, unexpectedly, I was given a book called *Ordinary People, Extraordinary Faith* by Joni Eareckson Tada. As I read
about her story and her strength, the fire for ministry was lit again,
and I started seminary, living out the reality that "greater is he that
is in you, than he that is in the world" (1 John 4:4, KJV).

In seminary it became clear to me that I was not like the others,
that somehow I was being called to something that did not look like
traditional vocational positions. That has only made my journey
that much harder. I found that every time I tried to be like everyone
else, I became unhappy and that made me restless. As I was willing to be challenged, willing to be with those at the margins and
to practice ministry alongside different faiths and denominations
as well as cultures, then I found something of peace and passion
renewed by working with diversity.

Honestly, I do not think I knew that I found my niche until I
was doing it. So many times people told me what I should be, but
because none of the roles fit, my efforts often felt like I was wearing
the wrong shoe. It was kind of scary because not until my last year
of seminary did I finally find a niche.

As in most seminaries, I was required to do some kind of chaplaincy program, and because I had a feeling I would like it, I decided
to go for the more difficult track known as clinical pastoral education (CPE). Now I am not going to lie and say that it was easy; it
was far from that. But it was about stories, and I got to sit with

people in the most uncomfortable places and listen. Strangers who had just met me would tell me their stories simply because I was willing to listen. Sometimes I just sat (or stood!) there for quite some time until they felt the need to unburden the thoughts within them. It was such an amazing experience. You see, I already knew that I enjoyed preaching, but because that put me in the light it wasn't my niche. I knew preaching was part of who I was and am, but as I walked with others, being there when death came, working with cancer patients, then I realized my ministry wasn't about my words but about my presence. I realized that I could do ministry *and* I could be Yana and live the story that Fanny Crosby sang:

> *Perfect submission, all is at rest,*
> *I in my Savior am happy and blest,*
> *Watching and waiting, looking above,*
> *Filled with His goodness, lost in His love.*

May we each live to tell the story and find our heart's desire.

NURTURING PASSION:
adventure and taking chances

LeQUITA HOPGOOD PORTER

The trouble is, if you don't risk anything, you risk even more.
—ERICA JONG, *FEAR OF FLYING*

How can you know what you're capable of if you don't embrace the unknown? —ESMERALDA SANTIAGO, *CONQUISTADORA*

I have searched for a meaningful activity for my life's work since the time I was a little girl, and I can say with the fullest confidence I have truly found it in this vocation. Although I found success in other work, including law and business, nothing prepared me for the joy and grace I discovered in being used by God to shepherd God's people. Ministry has opened up my creativity and passion for discovering and becoming fully who I am in God, and ministry has led me to use that passion to help others. It was not always so straightforward, though, and the journey took much longer than I ever anticipated at the outset.

This road toward self-fulfillment and actualization has taken many twists and turns. I started early in life with a hunger for knowledge, adventure, and exploration. I used to say, "I want to experience everything there is to experience in life!" I had a certain abandonment and fearlessness that was based in a high level of self-esteem and the knowledge that I was loved and appreciated by not only my family but also by God. This was constantly transforming my life.

Then, because of some strenuous and traumatic experiences I had as a child, my dreams were deferred for many years; my enthusiasm was almost destroyed, and I lived under a shroud of guilt and shame for too long. Yet, all the while I was in hiding, I was still learning and growing and seeking out the best of what I could be—but it was based in fear and feelings of inadequacy. Then I reached a point of no return. At the age of thirty, I reached a fork in the road that seemed to say to me, "You need to choose now either to live or die." By God's grace, I chose life.

Since that time I have been moving intentionally and methodically toward a fuller knowledge of who I truly am. My vocation, including all my interests, passions, and all that I have collected throughout my life, mean nothing unless I know deeply and profoundly who I am in God. Yes, I love preaching, I love teaching, I love poetry, I love the creative arts, and I have to say honestly, and I am pretty good at most of it. But I am at my best when I am helping people know themselves even more—to be more of who they truly are in God. And so, I love being stretched by experiences, I especially love being challenged and I gain strength from seeing others begin to explore and move toward their own destinies in life. I believe God is in the midst of it all. This is why my passion is to simply and fully *be*, and to help others to *be* as well, and the best *be* God has intended for us as individuals and in community.

Expectations run deep in my family. There is something about the immigrant experience that seems to deepen the responsibility and obligation the second generation carries within itself as a result of being descended of people who traveled far and long through many hardships to be in this country. I think that is a part of so many people's narratives whether they are first or tenth generation. It is the story of America, this becoming, this learning to be, and discovering who one is in the midst of promised opportunity and chances. But while that sounds lovely and wide open with possibility, it is limiting, too. It is frightening. The possibility for failure is overwhelming and can be paralyzing, especially when the script has been written for you all your life. To pursue medicine or law, to teach or be successful in business—these are part of the blueprints for a fulfilled life. But to pursue something unknown, and to create, inspire, and develop out of something unfamiliar—this is the beginning of becoming more, and becoming more who God wants of us. It is not easy. Sometimes it is lonely. But living into being God's own, God's creation, God's beloved is the ultimate risk, and it has the biggest returns. —MKK

My passion is fueled by years and years of dreaming and watching others succeed in their lives but being too afraid to step out and try something for myself. However, my passions grow with every expression of it in my life. They inspire me. So, I am convinced that our passions can be fully realized only when we are connected directly to our power source, which is God, and we lean and depend on God for everything, even every involuntary inhalation and exhalation.

I have learned and accepted with gratitude that this passion is a God-given passion, and I know with all my heart that it is fueled by God's spirit because there is no way I could do this on my own, or even by my own volition. And because of this gift I believe that I have to step out in faith, to take those risks, to take a chance on a God who has taken many, many chances on me. What joy and excitement and profound love I have experienced as a result.

In the past, I looked for my passion to be fueled by other people. I wanted acceptance and approval from others about things that gave me passion. Yet, when I did not get the approval, I began to lose interest in what I knew was important to me. It was all about getting other people to confirm what I already knew—and not just to confirm but, if possible, to endorse and participate in my pursuits. It took a long time to look within and find the source of passion there.

I am reminded of a lay ministry that I began at my home church in Summit, New Jersey, back in 1992. This was an empowerment ministry that exists to this day, which I was able to launch with the help of the women of the Fountain Baptist Church. I realized later that, when I first approached my pastor, I wanted him to launch the ministry; I would merely provide all the services and organization. He made it clear to me that it was *my* ministry to launch and to serve in. He made an announcement of our meeting, and then he stepped out of the picture. I was so upset with him at the time. But as time went on, I realized that he was doing what he was supposed to do in forcing me to do what God had called me to do!

I have many stories of passions and desires that I sought to place under a bushel when they seemed to be too hard. In seminary, I had a vision for something called "Project Princeton." The hope was to launch a new church in the area that adhered to basic Christian-Baptist principles, as well as incorporated a more ecumenical sense of worship experience for people of all races and cultures. I felt there was a need in the area, and I had worked on formulating the vision down to organizing and structuring programs and events. But I didn't feel qualified or passionate about becoming the church's pastor—frankly I was afraid! I tried to persuade a seminary profes-sor to pastor this church. I thought that this gifted and anointed preacher/professor would be the perfect pastor of this new church, and I promised him that I would do all of the organizational and administrative work to ensure that this was a church of excel-lence—the only kind of church that God deserves. I knew he had pastored before and was not interested in all of the pastor-type is-sues and challenges, and I agreed to take them all on if he would be the lead preacher and pastor.

I often think about this exchange that I had with this prominent man. And I often wonder what he was thinking as he repeatedly told me, "Why don't *you* be the pastor and the preacher? You have what it takes!"

More than ten years later, I was still struggling with seeing my-self in a pastoral leadership role. Probably the greatest obstacle I encountered in founding a church in Tampa, Florida, in 2005 was in struggling to believe that I was equipped for the task. The early days of that ministry were littered with insecurities and feelings of unworthiness. However, I worked, I studied, I served, and I did my best at everything I had to do in order to keep God's ministry alive and well. What was always surprising was that my greatest obstacle was myself and my lack of belief that God could use me in that way—just as God used so many others. But now I know, and I will never seek to hide my passion under a bushel, ever again!

NURTURING PLAY:
possibilities and seeing our lives as God's canvas

FELICIA DEAS

> When I used to think I wanted to be a children's pastor, a mentor (another woman who was a children's pastor) asked me, "Do you feel called to that because you REALLY feel called to it or because that's the only thing they've ever let you do?"
> —CHRISTINE HONG, INTERFAITH ASSOCIATE OF PCUSA

> Though we tremble before uncertain futures may we meet illness, death and adversity with strength, may we dance in the face of our fears. —GLORIA E. ANZALDÚA, POET AND SCHOLAR

It is ironic that I would be asked to write about my passion and finding my ministerial niche during what is shaping up to be a very dry season for me vocationally. There was a time when I was clear about my ministry. I wanted to be a pastoral counselor in a community setting. I would teach and offer lifestyle workshops as a part of a community center, as well as offer family and group counseling. I was passionate about helping people to help themselves and to discover the unfamiliar ways through which God has spoken to them in their daily lives. The desire to assist people in crisis still exists; however, I am still searching for the space within which that desire will be expressed fully.

~~~~~

> Once again letting go, submitting to the rule of God in my life and to God's sovereign care and providence even over my calling, and finding the space to live out that calling is always a challenge. It is humbling. I vacillate between feeling open and accepting to the current situation, and then flailing and floundering, almost throwing

a temper tantrum of sorts while demanding of God an answer to why there would be these passions in my life that I cannot carry out or pursue right now. God is patient with me, though. Like a child, after a while, I pick myself up and let myself get back on the slide or swing, to look around and see that the here-and-now is where God calls me right now. In doing so, in being open to playing with possibilities, I am awakened to Christ who is my justification, and the Spirit who sustains me, and my Creator who loves me. —MKK

There is a part of me that will always be drawn to hospital visitation and crisis intervention. I completed one year of CPE residency at a large public hospital in the city of Atlanta. I am grateful for the experience of being a spiritual leader outside the context of my congregation because it allowed me the opportunity to discover and construct a pastoral identity that was not controlled by the institution of the church. I enjoyed being with people in their time of need in the hospital. I believe there is a strong connection between health and spirituality. Illness, at times, affords us an opportunity to check in with our spirits about the alignment of the paths that we have been traveling in our daily life. Is how I am showing up in the world in harmony with my spirituality and how the world works?

I do not think it is by any coincidence that, as a young female minister, newly ordained and fresh out of seminary, I was committed to becoming the hardest-working, most compassionate, and most selfless minister to don a clergy shirt. I was determined to memorize Scripture and offer pat answers for the perplexing problems that my congregants faced. I was determined to mold myself into something that I was not in order to fit into what I felt the congregation expected me to be as a minister. It was tough. It was passionless. It was not me.

I was a generalist in two of my callings before I became a stay-at-home mom. This whole journey was entirely different from what I envisioned for my ministry. I understand, though, that ministry, both within and without a formal congregation, goes through seasons. And so, I carve out what I can in terms of ministry and my specific gifts in this space until another door opens up. My understanding of calling and vocation has broadened to include so much more than what it is on paper, and as a result, it has permeated every aspect of my life. Gone are vocational obligations where so much felt like fulfilling a job description. They are now vocational necessities. These include personal Bible study, connecting with others through fellowship and daily communion, and offering pastoral care in whatever situation, whether friend or stranger or my own children. My home is not my parish; rather, the whole world is my parish. What I have realized is that the possibility for ministry exists around every corner, and my job as an ordained clergywoman is to respond with courage and compassion. I believe that this more wholistic understanding of ministry comes out of growing up in an Asian culture, and a bit of understanding of yin-yang and balance. There is no need to compartmentalize or divide—ministry modeled after Jesus is thorough and constantly present. **—MKK**

Learning how to honor myself and how I show up in the world was one of the most rewarding lessons I learned as a minister. Instead of condemning my otherness as some secret shame, I've learned to allow my uniqueness to bless the world in which I minister. I believe facilitating that open and welcoming space is my gift as a pastor, because I can now teach from a place of knowing. This has become my passion—to create spaces within whatever context I find myself, spaces where people can feel safe to show up and live in the truth of who they are in God. I have created a ministry where I ask others to join me in releasing ourselves from the bondage of perfectionism, fear, and "we have always done it this way"–ism. Instead, I long to be open and responsive to a living God who wants to continue to co-create with us and through us.

NURTURING PERSPECTIVE:
contemplation and living out calling as seasons

LAURA MARIKO CHEIFETZ

Do work that matters. *Vale la pena.* —GLORIA E. ANZALDÚA, POET AND SCHOLAR

I tried to make my mind large, as the universe is large, so that there is room for paradoxes. —MAXINE HONG KINGSTON, *THE WOMAN WARRIOR*

I have a passion for leadership development, which is a direct result of the investment many put into my leadership development. In high school, I was part of a new church development (which sucked the joy out of church for me for a while) that used youth and children in worship leadership. Through that experience, although it was for better or worse (it was sort of damaging), I began to learn what it meant to be a leader in church. In college, I had lots of opportunities for leadership. I had professors who empowered me in leadership roles, as a teaching assistant and residential advisor, who took me and my classmates seriously. I now shudder to think that one professor left me her lecture to deliver, and I am sure it was a horrible experience for the class.

As a senior, I connected with the National Network of Presbyterian College Women (NNPCW), which is where the investment in my leadership development really took off, in tandem with my joining a local Presbyterian church, St. James Presbyterian in Bellingham, Washington. NNPCW put leadership in the hands of college women, and we were guided by a wise staff person, Gusti Newquist, who remains one of the coolest people I've ever met. Some of us in NNPCW started women's Bible study groups or women's college ministries. Some of us were pulled to engage with the wider church. Presbyterian Women (PW) sent me to India with a PW-elected leader to a World Council of Churches (WCC) Consultation on Women and Racism. The delegates in attendance, who hailed from all over the world, were respectful of me and the other young woman who was there, and I was pretty much hooked on global ecumenism. (I also stopped worrying so much about the future of the PC(USA).) My local church had older church members of multiple generations who engaged me respectfully and asked me to co-lead conversations on racism. I went to the adult Sunday school, which is where a whole bunch of retirees studied the lectionary texts of the day (me as a twenty-something and a bunch of seventy-year-olds).

I needed space to contemplate how God would form God's justice in me and what that would produce in my own life. I needed God to write and craft God's story of grace in my life, and I needed to be hospitable to that work in me. And so, I put off graduate school after college (thank goodness—it would have been the wrong choice for me) and served a year at the Presbyterian UN Office as Gender Justice Program Coordinator, then part of the Peacemaking Program. In that position, I also coordinated PC(USA) participation in the UN World Conference Against Racism (UNWCAR) in 2001. With the connections I made and those that my office helped me make, I ended up on the WCC delegation to the UNWCAR. I was treated very much as a colleague by Louisville staffers and by people in the United Nations non-governmental organization (NGO) and church communities in New York, which pushed me to grow up a little faster. In seminary, I was given many leadership development opportunities. The then-Vice President for Student Affairs, Mary Paik, made sure I had multiple opportunities.

What I learned from all the people who worked with me, opened doors, and invited me (or required me) to take on responsibilities for leadership was that I should not wait around for someone else to take care of shaping the next generation. I could step up now to do this in deliberate ways. I also learned that I should never be the youngest person in the room (which still happens far too often), and it may very well be up to me to make sure I invite that younger someone. We are facing some real challenges in the nonprofit world and in the church, where relatively few younger people of diverse backgrounds have been brought into leadership. I think this may be a change from previous generations, where churches and nonprofits were more willing to take on a young person and groom that person to be a leader, instead of demanding a finished leader upfront.

I took a nonprofit management course for my MBA, in which the professor looked at us and said his generation, the Baby Boomers, was worried that not enough of our generation was ready to step into leadership in the nonprofit sector. I got really frustrated with him, because I don't think the responsibility is completely ours. First of all, Gen X isn't that big a generation. Second, how is it possible to have young people ready for leadership if the Baby Boomers haven't made sure they are constantly inviting those young people to try out their leadership skills and coach us along?

I want my generation to have a fluid grasp on power. I want us to know what it means to share and truly collaborate with one another. I want us to be okay with something not being perfect but being exactly what was supposed to happen in that moment or season. I want us to give leadership development opportunities to young people, the Millenials, who are not yet completely ready. I want us to push to hire younger people and be willing to invest in them so they are ready for the big time. I want us to find ways to interact across generational lines so leadership development is something we enjoy and not something we take for granted and not something we assume is happening somewhere else.

I often wonder how my passions might change or how I might live them out as I get older, as God puts other callings in front of me, but I hope I never lose my commitment to developing young people. This is something that is a passion of mine, and more importantly, I believe it is one that is significant and essential to the church. Yet, there continues to be one major barrier: I walk into meetings where people say they do not know any young people right for a particular task. (Not everyone is committed to the ministry of developing young people for leadership.) I admit that I do not always know the "right" young people myself. However, we do already know young people; they exist, even if not in the pews every Sunday. We need to work a little harder to reach out to expand the network of people being tapped for leadership. Once we step out and allow God the room to open our eyes to those needs, and then to recognize the answers to our prayers, then we can write that story with God. The possibilities are endless.

Whatever the passion or calling and how it manifests itself in one's life, if we seek to be faithful to God's calling to us, we will be used to change someone's life in amazing ways.

> To love. To be loved. To never forget your own insignificance. To never get used to the unspeakable violence and the vulgar disparity of life around you. To seek joy in the saddest places. To pursue beauty to its lair. To never simplify what is complicated or complicate what is simple. To respect strength, never power. Above all, to watch. To try and understand. To never look away. And never, never, to forget. —ARUNDHATI ROY, *THE COST OF LIVING*

9

can you hear me now?

THE STRUGGLE WITH
VOICE AND AUTHORITY

CHENI KHONJE

> I love the LORD, because he has heard my voice and my sup-
> plications. Because he inclined his ear to me, therefore I will call
> on him as long as I live. —PSALM 116:1-2 (NRSV)

Voice is the distinctive manner or style with which one expresses
one's thoughts. Authority can be defined as the power to command
the attention of listeners as an accepted source of expert information on a particular subject. The combined exercise of voice and
authority has been challenged by those who find themselves con-
victed by the words that are spoken, in particular by those who
make them uncomfortable.

A plethora of historical accounts exemplify this statement. The
ones who are concerned with God-talk in flesh-and-blood realities
are of particular interest to me. Theologian Paul Tillich's discourse
on experiencing the New Being[1] brings to fore the notion of fully
engaging one's faith. The New Being, the new reality that has come
about through the person of the historical Jesus, opens our lives
to a new way of doing things. Participating in the New Being by
expressing one's religious calling as Christian, to share the gospel
of Jesus the Christ, is to accept a new vulnerability. This vulnerability is especially noticeable when the existential gauntlet is thrown

down by listeners who question the invitation to a more challenging experience of the New Being. Countless numbers who proffer a prophetic critique are challenged with the question, "Tell us, by what authority are you doing these things? Who is it who gave you this authority?" (Luke 20:2).

WHAT DO *YOU* KNOW?
finding my voice

Newly ordained to the ministry of word and sacrament, I would often run into situations in which my speaking was questioned by the hearer. In discussing the issue with several other female clergy, I soon learned that my experience was not unique. This discovery was at once disappointing and unsurprising given situations in which each incident arose.

Many newly minted female pastors initially experience the questioning of their authority when they encounter comments about their age. Discerning the spirit in which the remarks are made, one begins to hear a new set of questions behind the inquiries. "How is it that someone so young shows such wisdom?" The same skepticism and prejudice can be heard in the backhanded compliment that states, "You preach so beautifully, but how do you do it? You're too young to have experienced so much in life." More blatant is the comment, "Is there an online bank of sermons that pastors like you use to write and preach sermons?"

Several new clergywomen note that there is a time when church members generally accept that we are gifted as preachers. However, hurdles continue to be placed in our way as the congregation challenges the authority of a young female pastor in other areas of pastoral leadership. People generally accept that she has gone to seminary to prepare for a call to the pastorate. However, her knowledge of worship and music is often put to the test.

This issue came into sharp focus for me recently when I was questioned about my knowledge of hymnody at the church I was serving as pastor. I had asked the music director to have the choir sing "Dem Dry Bones" before I read the Scripture from Ezekiel 37. The story of the valley of the dry bones and Ezekiel's call to preach to them was the topic of my sermon. While I was preparing for worship that Sunday, I stepped into the choir rehearsal after the Sunday School class to chat with the organist. The director of music was flustered because one of the choir members, who happened to be on faculty of the local university's school of music, was questioning the choice of that musical introduction to the biblical text.

The professor was unfamiliar with the song and added in outrage, "It doesn't even have anything to do with your sermon. Why are you making us sing silly songs? Nobody understands the rhythm, and the congregation won't appreciate it either. Maybe you sang it in your country, but it is not anything that Americans would know."

One of the students in the class spoke up and said he remembered it from Sunday school, and he began to sing it. Others began to join in the singing because they recognized the song, although they commented later that they hadn't known its title. After they had sung the chorus, a second choir member, whose leadership was well-respected in the group, mentioned that it was a Spiritual. I agreed and asked if anyone knew about Ezekiel.

At this point the professor was quite flustered at being shown up, and repeated the complaint that the song had absolutely nothing to do with the Bible. I pointed out that the passage on which I would be preaching described Ezekiel's encounter with God. The professor told me in a loud voice that I neither had any knowledge of hymnody, nor did I understand how to ensure that the congregation would be familiar with the music that I selected for worship. I was then accused of choosing my favorite hymns from my home church in New York City and not taking into consideration that the congregation that I was serving had its favorites, too.

Trying not to embarrass the professor, who also happened to be an elder in the church, I quietly began to highlight the aspects of Presbyterian polity concerning the pastor's responsibilities in worship, such as selecting the Scripture to be read, handling the exposition and preaching of the Word, and choosing music for the service.[2] I pointed to the indices in the back of the hymnal that afford topical or scriptural allusions to aid in the choice of hymns. This elder was neither aware of the Book of Order nor informed about the tune, meter, topic, and biblical references in the Presbyterian hymnal.

It was soon time to begin the service, and as each hymn was sung, I could see the professor reading the bulletin and checking the back of the hymnal. When it came time to sing "Dem Dry Bones," the congregation members joined in the singing, clapping and doing the motions of the song. At the conclusion of the service, many of the parishioners exclaimed that they had not heard that song since Sunday school and were now happy as adults to make the connection with the Bible passage that inspired it. Congregants asked if I would use more Spirituals in the service because it lent a more multicultural feel to our worship experience.

The assumption being made by the congregation was that, because my skin was black, I would naturally know all the music sung in the African American religious tradition. When I intoned that I, an African, would be asking for their help as Americans who knew their own music they were flabbergasted.

"How would we know that music? Don't you know it?" one person asked.

I explained, "I was born in Africa, spent time in Europe, and then moved to the United States. How would I know all of the religious music that is available in the United States? See, we can work together on this: you tell me what you remember and I will research it and find the music." This proposal did not go very far, and it is probably a good thing that my parents had exposed me to a diverse selection of music that was both secular and religious in nature.

When I was asked to preach one of the seven last words at a joint service with African American clergy, to my dismay I again discovered that my voice as a female pastor was under scrutiny. These colleagues hailed from traditions such as the Baptist, Pentecostal, Apostolic, and Church of God in Christ (C.O.G.I.C.). Our group consisted of five male and two female pastors. I received a phone call from one of the male participants, and he began the conversation with an apology. The reason behind the preamble was revealed to be that the church at which the service would be held did not recognize the authority of women to preach. The first instruction for the day was that I was to sit to the side of the pulpit, away from the male pastors who would be seated on the dais. Second, I would not be referred to as Reverend or Pastor but as Sister. I informed him that I was not a Catholic nun and that they could either call me Pastor or dispense with that formality.

When I was given the word on which I would be preaching, I thought to myself, "Priceless!" I was to preach the fourth word, which is, "Father, forgive them; for they know not what they do" (Luke 23:34, KJV). It gave me a wonderful opportunity to teach in a Presby-costal[3] style. My sermon addressed the challenges of Christ's teaching about loving one's neighbor as oneself and the Pauline teaching that in Christ there is no east or west, no male or female. Just in case someone would say that the interpretation was based only on the New Testament, I also drew from the prophet Joel, who spoke for the Lord saying that both men and women would prophesy (Joel 2:28). Who then are mere mortals that we should question a woman's authority to speak or her gift of preaching when she has been called to the pastorate by God? My remarks concluded with asserting that God's truth remains the truth, no matter whether it is shouted from the mountaintops, taught from the pulpit, or preached on the floor of the church.

The sermon received resounding applause and a standing ovation. Several of my male colleagues came down from the dais and shook my hand, each whispering in my ear that if the service had been held at his church he would have asked me to sit with them. In the midst of the turmoil I was experiencing in my ministry, this was like a lifeline, an anchor, reassuring me that I was being faithful to God's call.

PREACHING WITH POWER:
finding my authority

It has been my privilege that the sermons that I have preached in a variety of churches have been well-received. This gift of preaching is often acknowledged by parishioners and guests who attend worship. When I preach prophetically, as a pastor I always hope that someone will say that the sermon has opened a new discourse that has challenged the hearer. I wait for the invitation to discuss what was said in the service and how the newly revealed understanding might be applied to Christian living.

I find it disturbing to hear the all-too-common quip in response to my (or anyone's) exposition of the Word: "What a good sermon, but then your sermons are always good," or "Wonderful preaching, you knocked that one out of the ballpark." The compliments are welcome, but reality hits when the message that I preach is lost somewhere between the times when the sermon is delivered to the lived experience of parishioners once they leave the church steps.

Worse still is the realization that the effect of past lessons has not been assimilated or applied to situations both within and beyond the walls of the church. Consider, for example, how we treat others, especially those who are on the margins of our community. When I hear stories about people who actively disengage from a ministry to the homeless, the incarcerated, the poor, or the addicted, I wonder what has happened with our ability to apply the words of Matthew 25:40 (NRSV), which state, "And the king will answer them, 'Truly I tell you, just as you did it to one of the least of these who are members of my family, you did it to me.'"

A colleague of mine was taken aback by such disengagement when her congregation asked her to cease and desist all mission activities in one of the impoverished Caribbean nations. For years she had been leading ministry teams, both from the church she served and others in the denomination, to work in this particular country. When my colleague asked for clarification, she was told that the people in that nation did not deserve the church's mission dollars; representative parishioners further explained to this pastor that the hurricanes and earthquakes that had devastated the country were a sign of God's punishment of the people living there.

It begs the question as to how we interpret the Lord's word, particularly when Jesus speaks about the greatest commandment and the second which is like it (Matthew 22:37-40). Jesus answers the question that was posed to him by the young inquirer by saying that believers should dedicate their whole being to loving God and their neighbor. This text is one that the lectionary does not miss, and so it is a passage with which people who claim to be lifelong Christians would be familiar.

Likewise, during my tenure at the church, the mission board proposed that we extend a welcome to those who were new in the neighborhood given the changing population in the immediate vicinity of the church I was serving at the time (with whom I continued to struggle with when it came to worship music). My facility with several languages had made my call to this particular pastorate an ideal one because of the match to the church's pledge to include outreach to the new members of the neighborhood. However, as my ministry progressed with the congregation I began to hear whispers that disturbed me.

One person in leadership took me aside and said, "Now we know that you have mentioned executing our mission plan, but only invite ten Hispanic families into the church. If you invite too many, we will be overrun because they have a lot of children and they will take over our church."

At first I was stunned by that statement and kept it close to my heart to pray over. I wondered if I was being hypersensitive or if the racist overtones that I was hearing were a misunderstanding on my part. After I had prayed for guidance on how to handle the situation, I was deeply troubled that the more I thought about the situation, the more starkly I saw the reality of what lay behind those words.

Needing to discuss the matter with the ruling elders, I prepared to present the issue as a pastoral concern. However, before I brought the matter before a meeting of the Session (board of leaders), I was accosted with a stern statement that nearly knocked me out of my seat. One of the ruling elders said to me, "I am disgusted. I am disgusted that you have a Spanish translation in the morning bulletin. And I am not the only person, because there is a whole group of us that feel this way. How dare you keep that in the bulletin?"

Asking for clarification, I asked the ruling elder to explain what he meant. I could not fathom that anyone would find someone else's language disgusting and was further dismayed by the answer. He claimed that it offended the people of the dominant culture in the church to see Spanish in the bulletin. He broadened the complaint by asking why we had to accommodate the other language when the official language of this country is English. In an effort to diffuse his anger, I smiled and pointed out that the United States does not have an official language, and if we were to start claiming that the language of origin of this country should be spoken, perhaps we ought to use Lakota (Sioux), Diné (Navajo), or Tsalagi (Cherokee). Then I proposed that if we were insisting on using languages of origin that I should perhaps preach in Hebrew or Greek depending on the text of choice for the sermon.

Curious enough to push a little further (and knowing that the Spanish translations had been part of the bulletin before I was installed as pastor), I asked when the church had started incorporating

Spanish in the bulletin and why they had elected to do so. According to their mission study, which they completed prior to beginning the process of calling a new pastor (namely, me!), the goal was to reach out to the Spanish-speaking families who were living in the immediate vicinity of the church. Employing the best pastoral guidance possible, I attempted to help the elders make the connection between the second greatest commandment that Jesus taught and reaching out in welcome to their sisters and brothers in Christ. Imagine my consternation when another ruling elder shot back, "They're not my brothers and sisters. I didn't choose them. Why should I have to welcome them? Don't they have their own churches?"

The visceral but unvoiced response I had to that statement was to wonder, *Then why did you bring me here?* I began to question silently how they felt about me and were we, the other black church member and I, just fulfilling a quota? Saying a quick prayer, I gathered my thoughts as I entered into this new teaching moment. I quoted their desire to grow as a congregation, and that while they often thought of themselves as friendly, their current inhospitable attitude would be a turn-off to the very people they sought to invite to join them. There was a serious divergence in what they had indicated as a primary ministry goal on their Church Information Form and what was happening in practice. The elders listened to the observations that I shared with them, but their body language and facial expressions spoke of future resistance that would be communicated in a passive-aggressive mode. Little did I know how this would turn out for me.

SHE'S NOT ONE OF US:
finding my pastoral identity

My voice has been brought into question in several other ways, but the one that I most frequently encountered was suspicion of my authority given my otherness. My ideas for ministry and the strategies I put forward for promoting spiritual growth in the congregation were often received with a jaundiced eye. Every now and then an elder would complain about a theological move that I made, asking, "Why are you bringing your Princeton ideas here to our church?

Maybe that works in your home church in New York City, but this is not that church."

It was disappointing to have to constantly defend perfectly logical ideas that were instantly misconstrued as ones that would work in urban and not rural settings. I finally got so tired of hearing that any Presbyterian polity or theological reasons employed were being dismissed because they were thought of as New York City ideas.

The accusation of "mistaking" the church as one that needed to be urbanized revealed another prejudice against or suspicion of the "outsider" pastor. One elder told me to my face that I was not to be trusted because I would steal the church's endowment. I quickly checked my feelings and drew on the pastoral skills that I had developed through Stephen Ministry training and reflected the question to him. I asked the elder if he realized that Presbyterian polity does not permit the pastor direct access to the church funds. The financial secretaries and treasurer were responsible for those transactions.

After consulting with the Presbytery, I discovered that a male interim pastor had tried to dissolve the church's funds for personal gain. At that point, I recognized that I needed to train the officers of the church on our church polity and how each of the boards, elders and deacons, should function. My hope was that there would be cohesive running of the church if we were all on the same page and shared information on who may handle the church finances and make decisions on how the funds are dispensed.

The resistance to being trained by a young pastor "who thinks we do not know how to be elders" was incredible. I still produced training manuals for each board; they were not used by the elders in the church, who openly admitted that they had not read them. However, the manuals were shared with other churches that have gone on to train their new officers using those manuals.

I CAN HEAR YOU:
finding my ministry

One of my colleagues with whom I spoke shared an encounter that she had with one of her parishioners. With her permission, I will note that she has a loud voice and has always had the ability to project it with confidence. She did not develop the gift of public speaking because she had taken speech and preaching classes at Princeton Theological Seminary; she already had the foundation for it in her personality. This wonderful preacher claims that her theological training enhanced her tone, pacing, and delivery in preparation for leading a congregation. Listen to her story, in her own words.

I've been ordained now for close to six years and yet it never ceases to amaze me that the most feedback I get concerns my voice. At the close of Easter morning worship recently, I was confronted by an older woman at the greeting line:

"I never heard you speak before. You gave those announcements so well."

"Thank you," I responded.

"That must be so beneficial as a woman. I mean, I could really hear you from where I was sitting!"

"Well, I've always had a strong voice. I believe it comes from my mother, who was a middle school teacher. You could always hear her from across the school!" I responded in a humorous tone.

"No, I mean in what you do as a woman. As a woman it's nice that you have a clear voice. That must really help up there."

Although well–meaning, the woman was impressed with my ability to welcome people to the church and lead the call to worship. Perhaps it was a fascination with a female pastor (the congregation has never had a female minister on staff). Or maybe it was a realization that a woman can lead, calling people to worship in a dynamic and confident way.

Whatever the reason, the disappointing reality for my own story is that even in the twenty-first century, it is still surprising/shocking/different to see a female in pastoral leadership roles.

—ANONYMOUS CLERGYWOMAN

This colleague communicated a second incident regarding inadvertent comparison to her former head of staff, who was a female minister with a dynamic preaching style. It was clear that this head of staff had connected with the content of her sermons and her emotions were clearly before the congregation. My friend, who was associate pastor, is honest and vulnerable, but in the preaching moment, she does not often get emotional. On one particular Sunday when she shared a story about offering pastoral care to the family of a young man who had just died in the hospital, my friend couldn't help but choke up as she remembered their interactions.

Following the service a congregation member came up to her and said, "Well, it's nice to see that you can be sad, too."

The comment hit her right in the chest. Implicitly, she was being compared with her head of staff's highly emotive preaching style without regard to her individual voice. She writes, "Apparently, my ability to express emotions was central to demonstrating the abilities that I possess in preaching the Word to the congregation." And, even more so, it struck her that if she didn't express such emotions from the pulpit, some hearers assumed that she did not connect with the story she was sharing with the congregation.

I often wonder when, if ever, I will stop being treated with suspicion or have my authority disregarded because of my age, color, and gender. One professor once said to me in seminary, "You need to find your voice."

Of course, he had assumed that only his dominant culture exists in the world and that all things considered should occur on his timetable. The fact that I come from a different culture in which we listen to our elders as they impart knowledge had not crossed his mind, even with his expertise in cultural anthropology. Having been brought up in an African context, even while living in Europe and the United States, I recognize that there is a time and a purpose for everything under heaven in much the same way as Ecclesiastes 3:1-8 teaches.

My voice was not lost; it has always been here with me, and therefore it does not need to be found. I choose when and how to use it. Perhaps it is even louder than many other women's voices because I am of Yao descent, a culture that is strongly matriarchal. The feminine, slightly accented timber of my voice is richly infused with an authority that comes from God. The difficult situations I went through both during seminary and during my time in ordained ministry so far have not hurt me or confused me. Rather, I am bolstered by God's presence in the community of supporters that surrounds me near and far. These encounters are not unique, and yet, I acknowledge that they don't happen to everyone. Thank God. For me, I see it as my lot in a way, a season, and one in which I believe I was faithful to God and to how God has shaped and created me. Like Paul, I'm not ashamed of the gospel and how that gospel has manifested itself in my life. I long to speak of it and preach it, and sometimes that brings unpleasant things to light, but it is God's grace that makes the difference.

It is the Lord's Word that I preach: Can you hear me now?

Notes

1. Paul Tillich, *The New Being* (New York: Charles Scribner's Sons, 1955), 15.

2. General Assembly, PCUSA, W1.4005 *Book of Order* (2011–2013), 85.

3. Presby-costal: a term that I coined in seminary. After I preached a fiery sermon, my Baptist friends commented that I could not possibly be Presbyterian. I told them that the Holy Spirit also fires up Presbyterians.

10

here i am

THE STRUGGLE WITH CALLING

MIHEE KIM-KORT

God has not called me to be successful. He called me to be faithful. —MOTHER TERESA, WINNER OF THE NOBEL PEACE PRIZE

It is a question I often am asked by church members, friends, youth group kids, college students, even strangers when they finally pick their jaw up off the floor after I tell them what I do for a living.

"How did you decide you would become a pastor/priest/minister?"

"What do you have to do to become a pastor/priest/minister?"

"Why did you become a pastor/priest/minister?"

"How did you know?"

How did you know you would become a pastor? How did you know God was calling you to be an ordained minister? How did you know it was right for you?

I never could tell if people were more shocked by my age, my ethnicity, or my gender. I could understand it to a degree. For some of us, growing up we never saw a woman pastor or preacher in the pulpit. There was no one to model ministerial leadership to us, no one who resembled us—as a woman, much less a woman of color—so the possibility of female pastoral identity did not even exist in our minds. For others of us, we witnessed women who were vocal from the pulpit and from every other platform in the community as they advocated for those who were voiceless and powerless in their congregations. Some of us tried to follow that newly beaten path made by trailblazers before us, and while the road made sense in some places, it posed its own difficulties in other spots.

Our different experiences say something about the Divine, that is, the wonder that God can be experienced and followed in numerous ways. It is difficult to deny the wideness of God's faithfulness to so many of us in so many distinct ways. And yet, despite our differences, whether in terms of ethnicity or culture, denomination or community, season or generation, out of these call stories we see surprising overlap in the process of being called to ministry.

COURAGE:
surrendering to the tension

People from my first home say I'm brave. They tell me I'm strong. They pat me on the back and say, "Way to go. Good job." But the truth is, I am not really very brave; I am not really very strong; and I am not doing anything spectacular. I am simply doing what God has called me to do as a person who follows Him. He said to feed His sheep and He said to care for "the least of these," so that's what I'm doing, with the help of a lot of people who make it possible and in the company of those who make my life worth living. —KATIE J. DAVIS, *KISSES FROM KATIE: A STORY OF RELENTLESS LOVE AND REDEMPTION*

In many stories about the call process, we hear over and over the various tensions that must be addressed during the inquiry stage—which is what Presbyterians call the ordination process. The equivalent in other traditions range from licensing to discernment, and all convey a sense of engaging the questions of one's journey, not only in the past but also the present and the future.

It was during my undergraduate studies. I was on the way to becoming a teacher. I had planned on teaching English literature to high school students. I loved my AP teacher when I was in high school and remember the way I felt in her class. But I was always involved in my church. I helped with Sunday school and youth group, and mission trips, too. It was a similar kind of work—being with young people and walking alongside them, teaching and mentoring them. It felt different though, too. There was a different kind of vulnerability being with youth and talking about their passions and struggles, and most of all, the experience of praying together. I started to realize it wouldn't be the same in the classroom. Then, I felt that tug toward full-time ministry. I saw that the gifts I felt I had for teaching could be carried over into ministry but the work would mean so much more to me. —ANONYMOUS AFRICAN AMERICAN CLERGYWOMAN

For some women, seeing the possibility of a different vocation in their future has been strange and problematic. Growing up they may have assumed or it was assumed for them that they would pursue one thing, whether it was in the family or a gift and interest discovered early on. Throughout their lives they may have had dreams to do something, anything, but ministry. Ordination was perhaps never on the radar, even if they grew up as active members in their churches. Becoming a clergywoman may have even seemed undesirable because of awareness of the extra barriers of gender, ethnicity, and other issues previously discussed in other chapters. Many of us wrestled with a variety of questions: "How am I going to explain this to our [insert influential family member here]?" "How am I going to get married and start a family?" "How am I going to find a church job?" "How am I going to explain this to my friends?" "How am I . . . ?"

But over and over we hear stories of how women pursued the call to ordination despite not having answers to all of these questions—no blueprints, no formulas, no issues resolved or anything figured it out. These women more than leaned into them. They lived into these questions and realized that God's call knows no bounds, and these tensions could not bind them.

We are unbinding our feet
We are women who write
We are women who work

We are women who love
Our presence in this world.
—*THE UNBOUND FEET*, 1979 PERFORMANCE AT THE SAN FRAN-
CISCO ART MUSEUM

~~~~~

I grew up never seeing a woman pastor much less a woman pastor who was also Asian or Asian American. But I did not really commit to the faith until college, where I joined a church-led fellowship. Most of my closest friends were also Asian American. We were all fairly traditional and conservative in our beliefs about men's and women's roles in leadership in the church. One summer I went on an extended mission trip in another part of the country. It was there I saw a woman preach, teach, and lead a church community. I had no clue what I would do after I got my college degree, but I felt something stir in me during this summer. This eventually turned into a desire to go to seminary, and when I began to pursue it, my close friends began to distance themselves from me. Now, after many years in ordained ministry, I am sad to say that we have lost touch. I know it is because they did not agree with my choice. Though I don't regret my choice to respond to God's calling to me, it took a long time to let go of my need for their approval.
—ANONYMOUS ASIAN CLERGYWOMAN

~~~~~

Although the tensions may never disappear from our lives, at some point in our journeys, most of us experienced moments when we could not avoid struggling with and facing those tensions anymore. We saw a choice before us. For some of us, it meant choosing between the more conservative seminary or the liberal divinity school to do our studies. For some it meant choosing to leave one denomination for another that embraced our call process. For some it meant choosing to lose the approval of our families and friends. For some it meant choosing to speak out about the inequities in ministry, not only in terms of gender but also in terms of ethnicity and culture within the wider church. For some it meant choosing to stay within their denominations, even though ordination for them was much more difficult. For some it meant choosing to be a prophetic voice in their home church about women in ministry.

For some it meant speaking out about issues of justice for other marginalized groups in their denominations.

But choosing did not and does not mean a static, linear process with clear-cut road signs. It does not mean saying something definitive that would be set in stone for all eternity. It means a dynamic engagement of the tensions experienced within our call, in our communities, in our particular seasons and being open to the possibility of rejection, refutation, and even modification. Choosing is not meant to be easy, nor will the choice necessarily always be "right," but the act of choosing can be a growing experience of power and agency, and one that shapes our journeys in a meaningful way. It is also a reminder of the ways God not only chose us for this vocation but also chooses us over and over despite what we choose or pursue in our lives.

Embracing the tension in our call process and even during ministry work is also a theological task, and one that is necessary—a vocational obligation. Among our many vocational duties one of the most central is to offer and embody hope. The very essence of hope might even be described as embracing the tension between living in a broken world and believing in God's redemptions, the tension between seeing the terrible inequities of the world and calling out for God's healing transformation, the tension between being questioned as a legitimate clergyperson and being an answer of God's light and love. What we do in the midst of those tensions is an expression of God's faithfulness and very presence in the world.

COMMUNITY:
surrendering to the inspiration

Therefore, since we are surrounded by so great a cloud of witnesses, let us also lay aside every weight and the sin that clings so closely, and let us run with perseverance the race that is set before us, looking to Jesus the pioneer and perfecter of our faith, who for the sake of the joy that was set before him endured the cross, disregarding its shame, and has taken his seat at the right hand of the throne of God. —HEBREWS 12:1-2 (NRSV)

In North American Christianity there is a renewal movement of emphasizing the centrality of community. This has surfaced recently in small missional or emergent communities, in home churches, and in faith-based fellowships. Many would argue, though, that community has always been an important component of Christian faith, from examples in the Bible both in the Old and New Testament, especially with the churches in Acts, to today's megachurches and their concepts of cell ministry or small groups. The point is that the relational aspect of church is a necessity in terms of one's faith identity and development. For clergywomen of color the imperative is even stronger even as it often is a struggle to find a community of those who experience the same hardships in the journey. Yet community can often be found and expressed in the most surprising ways.

I grew up seeing women preach from the pulpit. It was a part of our community, and I never questioned the validity of women in ministry. My mother is also a pastor, and I love to hear her preach and teach every Sunday. To me she is the best example of what it means to be faithful to God's call. She defies gender, in a way. She is obviously loved by all—men and women, young and old—and yet, this certainly does not mean she never deals with conflicts or dissatisfaction. But it is the way she cares for the people despite whatever opposition that says so much to me about what it means to truly be a pastor. I do not know anyone else who has as much integrity and fire as she does in her ministry to God's sheep.

—ANONYMOUS LATINA CLERGY

For some, the meaning of community is in witnessing the relationships between the pastor and the church. This shapes our notions not only of community but also of what it may mean to be a pastor. While for some the pastor-church relationship might involve negative associations—for instance, when the pastor is a dictatorial, tyrannical person who makes all the decisions for the church—for others, the relationship evokes only the best of human interaction and community, such as the woman who was inspired by the ways her mother embraced and embodied being a strong Latina woman pastor. Being genuine, be it culturally or personally, is often a theme in many of these stories. For some this meant letting go of the stigmas by larger society toward women of color, whether this means the woman is too loud or too quiet, too strong or too submissive, too intellectual or too emotional. For good or bad the community ultimately influences women pursuing ministry, whether it is through inspiration or admonition, through encouragement or challenge.

> Full-time ministry was never appealing to me. For one, the money was obviously not good. And second, I wanted to have a family someday and I just could not fathom how I would juggle children and ministering to people. Third, there were so many politics, and this always turned me off. But I never had an issue with seeing women in ministry. My church always supported women pastors. One Sunday my pastor—a male pastor—started to talk to me about ministry. I was very involved in ministry to children already. I loved their innocence and excitement. I loved the songs and stories and sharing stories from the Bible. It also made me want to know and learn more. So, I was encouraged to go to seminary. While I was in school my church continued to encourage me, even tell me I should think about ordained ministry. I never would have considered it without their support. And now, as a minister for about six years, with a family of my own and a husband who is also a minister, I know this was what I was meant to do for my life. It just took a community I trusted to tell me what was possible.
>
> —ANONYMOUS AFRICAN AMERICAN CLERGYWOMAN

It is truly a North American ideal to accomplish anything and everything on one's own. But in most other cultures, particularly Asian, African, and Latino communities in the United States, and especially in immigrant communities, there is a sense of radical collective. Even in the Korean language, our relationships almost define who we are because, when we talk to one another, we call each other by the name of our relationship (someone's mother or father, aunt, uncle, older brother, younger sister). I call my mother's sister *Imo* and my father's sister *Gomo*, and we have taught our children to call their father's sister, Sarah, *Gomo*. Even when we refer to ourselves as individuals, it's almost always in the plural "we" or "our," as in I would say, "our child, Desmond" rather than "my child, Anna." What this means is that we often need community to tell us who we are and what we are called to do with our lives.

Certainly, this is tricky. Larger society regurgitates to us that what corporations dictate should be a priority in terms of image and possessions (and vice versa). Often it is shallow, unhealthy, and completely about the self. In this case, we, as women, as women of color, as women of color created beautifully and wonderfully in God's image, have to reject what they say we must be or do in our lives; this is part of the resistance work of God's kingdom. Even in Christian communities there is abuse and violence by the authorities, or the larger community chooses to uphold beliefs that oppress especially women. The point of much of this book has been to address these very issues of negative manifestations of community. Nevertheless, ultimately God intended for community, the body of Christ, to be life-giving and life-changing.

I planned on getting a PhD in biblical studies. I am passionate about the Old Testament and wanted to teach in college or seminary. My childhood church had a few professors from the local seminary, and I always admired and respected them. Even though I had experience with female pastors I never felt totally comfortable with their preaching. I don't know why. When I went to seminary I was surrounded by other women who were pursuing ministry. I decided to take a preaching class where I heard many of them, and of course, I also had to preach. This experience changed my life. It made me want to do ordained ministry. The peers in my class encouraged me to do it, too. Now, as a pastor who preaches every week, even though some days are hard, I know it was God's call for me all along. —ANONYMOUS AFRICAN AMERICAN CLERGYWOMAN

The call process often opens us up to the varied possibilities of community. For me, it meant constantly redefining "family" and "home." For you, those concepts may embrace students in your classroom or a small group in seminary or a group of other clergy, both men and women. "Home" may be another church or another denomination or even another culture. "Family" may be your own congregation that you minister to now or a new group of friends. Like pastors, community comes in various shapes, sizes, and colors, and denominations, seasons, and contexts. But what is consistent in all these stories and conversations is that when the call is right we hear God's voice come to us through the community.

CALL:
surrendering to the passion

> Many people mistake our work for our vocation. Our vocation is the love of Jesus. —MOTHER TERESA, WINNER OF THE NOBEL PEACE PRIZE

Gut-wrenching and excruciating. At times the call process for women seemed akin to the drama of new love. There was the tug and pull, butterflies, and swooning, along with the fire of collisions here with two beings and two distinct wills who crash over and over into one another. Throughout it all, God's call was ultimately becoming the Beloved. Classes, degrees, exams, and filling our résumés were all good and fine, but what truly mattered was responding to God's call to be loved.

What I discovered to be the most important in this call process was allowing God's love to work in and through me. In some ways, it was a test of faith. It meant that if I truly wanted to follow God it would mean heartache and struggle. But, in the end, it was the beginning of really knowing God's love, and what it means to be a vehicle for God's love. —ANONYMOUS LATINA CLERGY

This was central to our clergywomen's identities. Race and gender, age and generation, culture and language were pieces to work through, but it was in the context of God's love, which would ultimately define not only our callings but also who we were to the core. Sometimes that would mean some kind of pain or agony, sometimes healing and transformation. But what needed to happen was an intentional surrender to God's love and passion, and what it would mean to be wrapped up in God's embrace as the source not only of our identities but also for our very lives. All that was a struggle that would not be meaningless but a part of our strength.

> Our deepest, most painful wounds not only leave us with scars that we bear forever, but also, if we make our peace with them, leave us wiser, stronger, more sensitive than we otherwise would have been had we not been afflicted with them. —RENITA J. WEEMS, *LISTENING FOR GOD: A MINISTER'S JOURNEY THROUGH SILENCE AND DOUBT*

Undeniably, the call process has shaped each of us. Some have been burned by it and left unable to recover and pursue ministry in the ways to which they felt initially called. Others have encountered few conflicts and surprising and beautiful expressions of community affirmation. What is consistent throughout these stories is the sense of the call process affecting our understanding of God—our faith experience, our spirituality, our theology. Despite the cultural differences between our ethnicities, whether some are stereotypically seen as strong-willed or submissive, vocal or quiet, authoritative or weak, the language of surrender, though taken in other contexts may seem negative, in this case is evocative of a revolutionary trust in God's promise, God's presence, God's provision.

> Like Jeremiah . . . I stammer and stutter and do all I can to walk away from the responsibility of unveiling the word of God. But, also like Jeremiah, I finish surrendering, praying . . . that I will speak with a clean heart, with purified lips. Yes, in the end I surrender and can only follow the command not to be afraid and to speak. The other side of the tension that holds me has to do with the sense that one should not preach what one does not live. No matter how hard I try to live according to what I am going to share with you, I fail time and again. I can only assure you that up to now in my life, each time I fail, and believe me it is often, I struggle to stand up. This struggle to stand up again and again, *la lucha*, as we refer to it in Spanish, seems to be what marks the rhythm of my living. The struggle is not to go through life bent

on not falling. No, the struggle, *la lucha*, is to learn to stand up again. There is no possibility of really picking oneself up, of really going on, if one is not willing to be converted. You see, what we have to realize is that each falling down is a calling to be converted, to become more fully ourselves, and that we cannot do it if we simply get up and go back to the same way of being that led us to fall in the first place. —ADA MARIA ISASI-DIAZ, PROFESSOR AND THEOLOGIAN

Clergywomen of color share much in common in terms of the struggle in our calls and ministries with our Anglo sisters. And yet, the layers of experience are complicated in such a distinct way that it behooves us to offer these unique stories as a continuous challenge to the wider church. The more possibilities we can embody as expressions of Christ the farther and deeper will be the reach of God's kingdom. May God bless all our rising and falling together, all our struggles and successes, and our journeys, for the sake of God's glory.

epilogue

We are the ones we have been waiting for. —ALICE WALKER,
AUTHOR, ACTIVIST, POET

I know a little something about waiting.

I waited to go to seminary.

I waited to meet the one I would marry someday.

I waited to receive God's call to ministry.

I waited for one church to believe in me enough to ordain me
and then to hire me.

I waited to have a family.

I waited for my second pregnancy, and my third child to come
into this world.

I look down in my lap, and my third-born is asleep. This project
was born more than a year ago when he was not even a glimmering
in anyone's eye. I am not supposed to be able to conceive without
medical intervention, and yet all of a sudden, here he is, snoring,
eyes fluttering a little, hands clenched in fists near his impossibly
huge jowls. I remember when we first found out we were pregnant
with him, and it was a certainty and not a concern about ectopic
pregnancy or some other abnormality. I was in the midst of putting
the finishing touches on my first book, the prequel to this dream,
and beginning to put together some thoughts about how to craft a
space for these stories to reside in order to nourish not only me but
also others like me. Birthing this project was not too unlike birthing my third child: full of surprises, unexpected delight, and more
lessons learned (some I thought I had already learned in another
season).

So, while he was swimming, growing, and changing in utero, I was writing and pursuing writers, and we formed a small community. Some I knew well, and others I have never met in person, as we connected only through the occasional phone call. Most of our exchanges were done electronically. Yet somehow I feel tightly and steadfastly knit with these other women. Not only have I been encouraged and inspired by each woman and story, but also I have been fed like never before. I have had my thirst quenched in plentiful ways. I, too, swam in those waters, growing and changing, and seeing so much more.

It is another baptism of sorts—one that is not done decently and in order as the good Presbyterians would have me do with a little sprinkling, but where I cannonball into the waves like I am a kid on summer vacation. Full immersion, like my Baptist and Anabaptist sisters, but instead of a quick dunking, I play, I splash, and I float on my back, look up at the sky remembering that I am made of dirt and water, and that is divine. That baptism reminds me it is God who calls and shapes me because God loves me. And so I want to work much harder for the sake of our little ones and for the sake of God's peaceful and hopeful kingdom helping to shape its citizens so they are truly loved, too.

As I finish polishing this manuscript as much as possible, I let myself savor the stories in these pages like a glass of fine water turned into wine from that wedding at Cana. I celebrate, I give thanks, and I am deeply humbled by all the sacrifices and risks made by these writers. These clergywomen were vulnerable. They were transparent. They were genuine. And they were and are trustworthy. These are only glimpses into much more complicated histories and larger narratives. Yet even these small windows allow us to see the possibilities for real connection and community, a little taste of the kingdom of God and how we experience that in the midst of struggle and surrender, in those places where reconciliation with God, neighbor, and self is rooted in embracing the other.

Being the other is not only a philosophical, social, political, or literary concept; it is a theological image. It speaks of a God of the margins, a God for the oppressed, a God who loves and pursues the stranger. And despite the history behind it and how it traditionally is a negative phenomenon, being the other does not have to be associated with colonial and imperialistic movements or a tool of oppressors or a burden of those who internalize what it means for the oppressed. The language of the other is redeemable but also an instrument for redemption. It speaks of the extreme and miraculous routes God forges to connect to us. It is the other that helps us to see God's love for us even more. It is when we see and recognize the other in ourselves that we begin to fathom the depths of God's love for us.

And so, it is once again those streams that sculpt the mountain from the bottom up to the top that hint at this divine reality. Rather than waves and rapids that rush by a lovely but complex terrain, these streams that run uphill lovingly perceive and shape each rock, each tree, each inch of the ground. Likewise, I see these stories in the same way and am blessed by how they have shaped not only my identity and vocation but also my faith. I would not want my life to be any other way, for surely struggle and surrender go hand in hand when it comes to following in the way of Christ. It is that struggle that will always connect me to humanity more so than anything else, and it is the struggle that makes me realize how valuable this work is in the world, and that while we struggle together, walking hand in hand, singing those songs of protest, resistance, and revolution, God walks in our lines, too.

All struggle, all resistance is—must be—concrete. And all struggle has a global resonance. If not here, then there. If not now, then soon. Elsewhere as well as here. —SUSAN SONTAG, *AT THE SAME TIME: ESSAYS AND SPEECHES*

afterword

At an event I participated in many years ago, a friend of mine stood up and shared who she was, what she had experienced, and how she felt. Later, she said she did this so that she would be present in the room. Her witness and her testimony encouraged me to be to follow her example and to also boldly stand and share myself with others. It was a way of self-naming and identifying who we were, in that space, in that moment, as young women who had been devalued in our contexts. And, though it was risky and scary, it was also empowering and freeing. Sharing in community gives those in the center a chance to experience the gifts, strength, courage, and love from those in the margins.

This may just be why *Streams Run Uphill: Conversations with Young Clergywomen of Color* was written—to make visible what would otherwise remain hidden, that is the thoughts, challenges, pain, and joys of being young clergywomen of color in this emerging era. Mihee Kim-Kort's writing is reflective and poetic; it flows over you like a refreshing waterfall. Contributors to this work add their voices to hers, offering rich reflections on their years of experience navigating racial, cultural, and gender differences in their churches and ministry contexts.

As Mihee writes, "There are stories about the heavy burden we carry because of the color of our skin and what it means to confront our identity with congregations that both contrast with us and mirror us. There are words about what we have gleaned from our own lives—hard lessons, and ones that continue to surprise us season after season" (p. ix). We categorize people by arbitrary human distinctions such as race, even though evidence indicates that the genetic code for all human beings is essentially identical. As Laura Mariko Cheifetz suggests, "I do not believe all these categories are real.... However, I believe these categories have real consequences for our society, our identities, the ways in which our political process functions, and our access to resources" (p. 45).

Streams Run Uphill is an important resource, not only for women of color but also for others who serve in the church. As church organizations set goals to grow multiracial and multiethnic congregations and to partner with young adults to serve Christ in the world, new generations of culturally diverse clergywomen are boldly declaring the church's great need for cultural competency in all levels of the church. This cultural competency will not come without church leaders moving past surface-level conversations to deeper engagements, sharing personal stories, and risking getting to know each other across traditional lines of gender, generation, race, and culture. That is what this book asserts.

Streams Run Uphill names, affirms, and makes visible the experiences of young clergywomen of color. As Mihee suggests, "Often women of color experience what I call a double silence. It is not only one's skin color or ethnicity but gender that doubly binds us up and causes us to be invisible to the wider culture" (p. 61). It is my hope that the voices shared in this book will shatter the silence, and that the church will appreciate and value the beautiful image of God as seen in young clergywomen of color, who faithfully serve in our churches. This work is an effort to show what is unseen, to share personal stories, and to join with our sisters of color in redemptive ministry in the church of Jesus Christ.

Rev. Dr. Rhashell Hunter
Director of Racial Ethnic and Women's Ministries
Presbyterian Women of the General Assembly Council
Presbyterian Church (USA)

the writers

LARISSA KWONG ABAZIA is an ordained minister in the Presbyterian Church (USA). She received her bachelor of arts from Rutgers University (2003) and her master of divinity from Princeton Theological Seminary (2007), both in New Jersey. She serves as pastor of the First Presbyterian Church of Forest Hills, a multicultural, multiethnic congregation located in Queens, New York. She and her husband, Dan, have one son. She enjoys being with her family and friends, exploring new places, finding great restaurants, trying new foods, cooking, and reading.

RUTH-AIMÉE BELONNI-ROSARIO is an ordained minister in the Presbyterian Church (USA). She received her master of divinity from Princeton Theological Seminary. Currently, she is associate director of admissions at Princeton Theological Seminary. She is married to a minister and spends much of her time reading, exercising, and serving churches in multiple capacities. She loves preaching, traveling, warmer climates, and walking along the shoreline.

LAURA MARIKO CHEIFETZ is an ordained minister in the Presbyterian Church (USA). She received her master of divinity from McCormick Theological Seminary and her master of business administration from North Park University. Currently, she is director of strategic partnerships at The Fund for Theological Education. She enjoys spending time with friends over food, exploring whichever region in which she happens to live, and still believes *The Wire* is the greatest television show in history.

FELICIA DEAS is an ordained minister in the Pan African Orthodox Christian Church (UCC). She received her master of divinity from Candler School of Theology at Emory University. Currently, she is associate pastor at Shrine of the Black Madonna in Atlanta, Georgia, and a victim witness advocate for the office of the Fulton County district attorney. She has three children and enjoys spending time singing, dancing, and planning escapes to the Caribbean islands.

BRIDGETT A. GREEN is a doctoral candidate in New Testament and Early Christianity at Vanderbilt University. She is a teaching elder of the Presbyterian Church (USA). Prior to pursuing her doctoral studies, Bridgett served in various capacities among the ministries of Racial Ethnic and Women's Ministries/Presbyterian Women in the Presbyterian Mission Agency. She preaches and teaches nationally for various conferences, congregations, and gatherings on the New Testament, women's ministries, and multiculturalism.

CHENI KHONJE is an ordained minister in the Presbyterian Church (USA) and is currently serving a congregation in Dunkirk, New York. She holds a master's degree in microbiology and graduated from Princeton Theological Seminary with a master of divinity. She is currently pursuing a doctor of ministry with a concentration in preaching at Lutheran Theological Seminary in Philadelphia, Pennsylvania. Cheni loves to travel, knit, cook, and learn different languages, and she is an avid football and hockey fan.

MIHEE KIM-KORT is an ordained minister in the Presbyterian Church (USA). She received her master of divinity and master of theology from Princeton Theological Seminary. Currently, she is the staff person for UKIRK at Indiana University, where she works with college students. She is married to a minister and has three children, and she spends much of her time reading, writing and blogging, and dreaming about food trucks.

ERICA LIU is an ordained minister in the Presbyterian Church (USA). She received her master of divinity from Princeton Theological Seminary and her undergraduate degree from the University of California, Berkeley. She currently serves as campus co-pastor at Pres House, the PCUSA campus ministry at the University of Wisconsin, Madison. She shares and leads this ministry with her partner, Mark Elsdon, who is also an ordained minister. Together they have two children.

YANA J. PAGAN was ordained by the American Baptist Churches USA in 2008. She earned her master of divinity from Palmer Theological Seminary in Philadelphia, Pennsylvania. Having served as a hospice chaplain and as an associate pastor, she is currently an adjunct professor of justice at Esperanza College of Eastern University. She also serves local ministries, including work as coordinator of the afterschool program at The Simple Way, an alternative community founded by activist and author Shane Claiborne in urban Philadelphia.

LeQUITA HOPGOOD PORTER is an ordained minister in the Baptist church, as well as a licensed attorney and business consultant. She received a master of divinity from Princeton Theological Seminary, a master of business administration from Rice University Jones Graduate School in Houston, Texas, and a law degree from the University of Cincinnati College of Law in Ohio. She currently serves as first female pastor of the 170-year-old East Preston United Baptist Church of Nova Scotia, Canada. She was also founding pastor of the Kingdom Bible Christian Church of Tampa, Florida. She is married to William Porter, and together they have two children and one grandchild. They now reside in Dartmouth, Nova Scotia.